50 SWEDISH COFFEE BREAKS

SHORT ACTIVITIES TO IMPROVE YOUR SWEDISH ONE CUP AT A TIME

COFFEE BREAK LANGUAGES

Activities developed by

HANNA JEDH

Introduction by

MARK PENTLETON

Series Editor

AVA DINWOODIE

CoffeeBreak
Swedish

First published by Teach Yourself in 2023
An imprint of John Murray Press
A division of Hodder & Stoughton Ltd,
An Hachette UK company

1

A CIP catalogue record for this title is available from the British Library

Paperback ISBN 9781399810449
eBook ISBN 9781399810456

Typeset by KnowledgeWorks Global Ltd.

Printed and bound in Great Britain by Clays Ltd, Elcograf S.p.A.

John Murray Press policy is to use papers that are natural, renewable
and recyclable products and made from wood grown in sustainable
forests. The logging and manufacturing processes are expected to
conform to the environmental regulations of the country of origin.

John Murray Press
Carmelite House
50 Victoria Embankment
London EC4Y 0DZ

Nicholas Brealey Publishing
Hachette Book Group
Market Place, Center 53, State Street
Boston, MA 02109, USA

www.teachyourself.com

In memory of
Lovisa Arnesson-Cronhamre

CONTENTS

FIKASUGEN?

Hej! Fikasugen? Fancy a coffee? This book is designed to make it easy for you to learn just a little bit of Swedish every single time you take a Coffee Break.

It is divided into three sections, so that you can decide how long you've got and choose an activity that will fill whatever time you have. Is it just a quick **snabbfika**? A little longer for a **påtår** or a **långfika**? Do you have time for a piece of **prinsesstårta** to go with that? Whether you have 5, 10 or 15 minutes for your Coffee Break today, we have something to accompany your refreshment.

Throughout the book, you will find a variety of activities, including reading texts, grammar exercises, writing tasks, idiomatic explanations and vocabulary practice.

Simply decide how long you have, choose an activity from either the 5-, 10- or 15-minute Coffee Break section and start learning. **Nu börjar vi!**

ABOUT COFFEE BREAK LANGUAGES

Coffee Break Languages came into being in 2006 with the launch of the Coffee Break Spanish podcast. As the first podcast for beginners in Spanish, the idea of "learning a language on your coffee break" quickly took off, and soon learners around the world were using the Coffee Break Languages podcasts and online courses to build their language skills.

Since then the Coffee Break method has grown to cover nine languages and has been recognised through numerous awards, including European Professional Podcast of the Year and the European Award for Languages.

The Coffee Break Languages team of language experts, teachers and native speakers is led by Mark Pentleton. A former high school languages teacher himself, Mark continues to share his passion for language learning, and the opportunities it provides, with learners around the world through podcasts, videos, courses and books.

INTRODUCTION
THE IMPORTANCE OF PRACTICE

MARK PENTLETON

"You've got to learn your instrument. Then you practise, practise, practise."

It was the virtuoso jazz saxophonist Charlie Parker who outlined the importance of practice in this way. Indeed, in a 1954 interview with fellow musician Paul Desmond, he explained that, over the course of three or four years, he would spend up to 15 hours a day practising. This allowed him to master the improvisation skills which then led to the development of bebop and influenced countless musicians who came after him.

No matter what skill you are acquiring, regular practice plays a crucial part. And don't worry, we're not suggesting 15 hours a day! You may well bake several hundred croissants before becoming confident in your ability to master the recipe. If you're doing the Couch to 5K running plan, you need to train regularly before you're ready to tackle those 5,000 metres. And if your child happens to be learning to play the violin, then the old adage of "practice makes perfect" is probably something you say on a daily basis.

Your "instrument" is the Swedish language. You can already play some notes on the instrument, and perhaps you can even manage a few tunes. You're probably at the stage now of wanting to "perform" these tunes, using the Swedish you know in spoken and written situations, and perhaps even move on to more complex pieces. But before you reach this stage, there's something you must do. You've guessed it: practise!

As I said, there's no need to follow the same intense practice schedule as Charlie Parker, spending many hours a day on your language skills. Indeed, since our very first Coffee Break Languages lesson back in 2006, we've stressed the importance of "little and often" when it comes to improving your language skills. And that's exactly what this book is about.

We've brought together a collection of interesting and enjoyable exercises which will help you build your vocabulary, increase your understanding of grammar and develop a cultural awareness, all within the space of a "coffee break".

Through the exercises, you'll learn new words, see examples of grammar points that you know and learn new constructions. You'll complete reading challenges, acquire new idiomatic expressions and learn to describe what you see in a photo, a skill which you can take into your daily life and practise your language wherever and whenever you want.

If you're training for a marathon, there's no doubt that the practice you put in beforehand is hard work. But language learning is not a marathon: it's a stroll in the park, a walk along a beach at sunset, or a drive along a beautiful lakeside as the early-morning mist clears. By ensuring that your practice is enjoyable, you'll make faster progress and you'll benefit from deeper learning. And that's exactly why we've written this book of fun and engaging exercises.

I started the introduction to this book with a quotation by Charlie Parker. However, I didn't give the full quotation. Having established the fact that, after learning the basics, what you need to do to master an instrument is "practise, practise, practise", Charlie Parker went on to add a third stage in this process:

> "And then, when you finally get up there on the bandstand, forget all that and just wail."

That, in a sense, is what we're all aiming for as language learners. Of course, "wailing" may sound unpleasant and conjure up images of tears and despair, but in the context of jazz music, Parker was suggesting that, if you've learned the tune and practised over and over again, then you are ready to fly, enjoying the moment and letting the music flow naturally. When you have completed all of the exercises in this book, I hope that you will feel ready to "fly", "wail" or simply enjoy the moment, letting your language flow naturally using the new words, phrases and grammar points you've practised.

So, all you need to do now is decide how long you'd like to spend on your Swedish today, pick any of our coffee-break-length exercises, and begin your practice. I wish you "happy language learning" and, of course, "happy coffee breaking"!

HOW TO USE THIS BOOK

The activities in this book vary slightly in their difficulty from one to the next, but are generally around lower intermediate level, or A2–B1 on the CEFR. Remember that even if you find a particular activity a little easier, consolidation is a vital part of language learning and no learning is ever wasted.

CHECKLISTS

At the start of every section of the book you have a checklist where you can record your Coffee Breaks by ticking off activities as you complete them.

WRITING SPACE

✎_____ This pencil followed by a line indicates a space for you to write your answers. Of course, feel free to add your own notes in any blank spaces on the pages too.

ANSWERS SECTIONS

At the end of each activity, we'll tell you which page to turn to if there is an answers section. Take your time to read the examples and explanations that we give you. If there are words or phrases that are new for you, remember to use your dictionary to help you. You can use any space on the page or your own notebook to write this new vocabulary and help you remember it. There are also some extra pages at the back of this book where you can write your own notes.

TYPES OF ACTIVITY

Each of the three sections of this book contains a number of different types of activity. Below, you'll find a description of each type, so that you know what to expect every time you choose an activity. Whether you're looking for some reading practice, a writing task, some help with grammar, or something else, we hope that these descriptions help you to decide how you're going to spend each Coffee Break.

5-MINUTE COFFEE BREAKS

Word Builder

In these activities, you will learn some interesting pieces of vocabulary on a variety of topics. There is then a short exercise to allow you to practise this vocabulary in context. To make the most of the Word Builder activities, we recommend writing down the words that are new to you in your own notes to help you remember them.

Mini Grammar Challenge

These challenges are designed to give you a little extra practice of some tricky Swedish grammar points. Each activity will focus on one specific point and will include a brief explanation, an exercise and answers.

Idiomatically Speaking

In each of these activities, we will focus on one Swedish idiomatic expression. First, we will explain the meaning of it and provide some examples of some of the contexts in which the idiom can be used. Then, there will be a short exercise or space for you to practise using the idiom in your own sentences.

Say What You See

In these writing activities, we will provide some suggested phrases to help you write a description of an image. As there is no set answer for this type of exercise, you may not know whether or not what you've written is entirely correct. Don't worry about this too much, however, as the purpose of these writing activities is simply to get you writing freely in Swedish, practising creating different types of texts and, in this way, developing your writing skills. For these activities, we have included our own "answer", which we hope you will find useful to see. However, it's important to remember that there is no single correct answer, so don't worry if your description is very different.

Guided Translation

Each of these activities is based on a short piece of text in Swedish: a famous quote, a saying or a joke. We will talk you through the language used in the piece of text to examine in detail the vocabulary and structures used and to help you come up with a good translation of it.

10-MINUTE COFFEE BREAKS

Translation Challenge

In these activities, your challenge is to translate sentences from English into Swedish. There will be hints to help you, if you need them, and suggested translations and language explanations in the answers section.

Famous Swedish Speakers

These are designed to help you develop both your reading skills and your cultural knowledge. They are based on texts about famous Swedish speakers and include a vocabulary list and questions to help you test your understanding of the text.

Jumbled Letters

In these activities, you will be given a definition of a word in Swedish and an anagram. Your task is to unscramble the letters of the anagram to find the word being defined. Then, test your knowledge of the language by seeing how many other Swedish words you can make using those letters.

Number Focus

It takes a while, when learning a language, to reach the stage where you can instantly visualise the corresponding digit when you hear a number being said out loud. This can only become easier with practice, which is why our Number Focus activities include a variety of exercises, all designed to help you practise your numbers in Swedish.

Taste Bud Tantaliser

These activities use recipes as reading texts and include a vocabulary list and a reading comprehension or language exercise, so that you can practise your language skills while learning about a dish from Sweden. While the activity should only take around 10 minutes, there's nothing stopping you from getting to know the language in the recipe even better by following it and making the dish yourself when you have more time!

15-MINUTE COFFEE BREAKS

Reading Focus

These longer reading activities will allow you to study a short text about a particular aspect of Swedish culture. They include a vocabulary list, comprehension questions and language questions.

Vocabulary Consolidation

This is a vocabulary drill exercise that will help you to familiarise yourself with pieces of vocabulary on a specific topic. Each activity focuses on 20 pieces of vocabulary and includes a number of different exercises to help you practise and get to know them.

Grammar Focus

While the 5-minute Mini Grammar Challenges are perfect for a short bit of practice of specific grammar points, in these Grammar Focus activities we take a more in-depth look at different topics in Swedish grammar, providing a more detailed explanation and a number of different exercises to help you practise.

5-MINUTE COFFEE BREAKS

CHECKLIST
5-MINUTE COFFEE BREAKS

Say What You See

Guided Translation

VILKET VÄDER!
WORD BUILDER

Vilket väder! ("what weather!") is a useful exclamation to know in Swedish. It means that it is either very good or very bad weather. Swedish weather involves great contrasts – dark, harsh winters and often dry, bright summers with long days and short nights. Swedes generally care a lot about weather and the seasons, as they have an impact on mood and activities. So, it's important to know how to talk about the weather in Swedish! Let's learn some useful vocabulary now.

* * *

(en) sol - sun
blåsigt - windy
snöar - snowing
mulet - cloudy
kallt - cold
varmt - warm
(ett) moln - cloud

dimmigt - foggy
(en) åska - thunder
regnar - raining

Here are some example sentences using this vocabulary. When speaking about weather, we always use **det** ("it") and -t endings on adjectives.

> **Solen skiner och det är varmt i luften.**
> *The sun is shining and the air is warm.*

> **Det ösregnar och det är jättekallt.**
> *It's pouring down and it's really cold.*

> **Det var kallt på morgonen men nu skiner solen.**
> *It was cold in the morning but the sun is shining now.*

> **Det snöar idag.**
> *It is snowing today.*

Låt oss öva! Now, practise using some of this new vocabulary by writing your own sentences on the lines below. Pick three locations around the world that you have visited or would like to visit and write a sentence for each, describing in Swedish what you think the weather may be like there today.

_____

_____

_____

_____

_____

_____

_____

_____

_____

_____

2

VILKEN, VILKET ELLER VILKA?
MINI GRAMMAR CHALLENGE

As you already know, a lot of Swedish grammar depends on the article of the noun in the sentence. For example, adjectives change their endings depending on whether the noun they are describing is an **en** noun, an **ett** noun or is plural. The same rule applies if you use the question word "which". Read the short explanation and examples below, then complete the exercise that follows to practise when to use **vilken, vilket** and **vilka. Nu kör vi!**

* * *

In Swedish, the word for "which" depends on the noun that follows. **Vilken** is used for **en** nouns, **vilket** is used for **ett** nouns and **vilka** is used for plural nouns.

Let's take a look at some examples:

Vilken är din favoritlåt?
Which song is your favourite? / What is your favourite song?

Vilket är ditt favoritgodis?
Which sweet / candy is your favourite? / What is your favourite sweet / candy?

Vilka är dina favoritartister?
Which are your favourite artists? / Who are your favourite artists?

Note that while in English we can ask "what is your favourite song?" or "who are your favourite artists?", in Swedish we use **vilken / vilket / vilka**, so we're really saying "which is your favourite song?" or "which are your favourite artists?"

It's important to know that **vilken, vilket** or **vilka** can also be used in exclamations. For example, in English we would say "what awful weather!", but in Swedish this would become the equivalent of "which awful weather!" – **vilket hemskt väder!** We use **vilket** here because **väder** is an **ett** noun.

EXERCISE 1

Nu övar vi! Based on the answers provided, fill in the gaps with the correct word for "which" – **vilken, vilket** or **vilka** – in each question.

1. Q: ✎_____ hus bor Tora i?
   A: Hon bor i det stora vita huset bredvid tågstationen.

2. Q: ✎_____ land kommer du ifrån?
   A: Jag kommer ifrån Norge.

3. Q: ✎_____ universitet går du på?
   A: Jag går på Uppsala universitet.

4. Q: ✎_____ språk talar du?
   A: Jag talar både svenska och finska.

5. Q: ✎_____ är din favoritfärg?
   A: Min favoritfärg är röd.

EXERCISE 2

Match the statements to the correct response.

1. Vilken trevlig lägenhet!	A. Varsågod, du är väl inte allergisk?
2. Vilket ljuvligt väder!	B. Eller hur? Hon är min favoritförfattare.
3. Vilka fina blommor!	C. Visst är de? De heter Ludde och Ronja.
4. Vilken fantastisk bok!	D. Tack, jag har nyss flyttat in i den.
5. Vilka söta hundar du har!	E. Ja, inte ett moln på himlen.

* * *

Bra gjort! Once you're happy with your answers, turn to page 60 to check them.

ATT SITTA MED SKÄGGET I BREVLÅDAN
IDIOMATICALLY SPEAKING

Have you ever "sat with your beard in a letterbox"? Probably not many of us have – it certainly doesn't sound like a very positive experience! **Att sitta med skägget i brevlådan** literally means "to sit with the beard in the letterbox", but it is an idiomatic expression that describes being stuck in a tricky or embarrassing situation. Here are some examples of this expression in context:

> **Hon hade lovat både Lena och Fredrik att gå på bio men satt med skägget i brevlådan när båda dök upp samma dag.**
> *She had promised both Lena and Fredrik that she would go to the cinema with them, but it was embarrassing when they both turned up on the same day.*

> **Jag kom försent till jobbet och chefen var redan där så då satt jag med skägget i brevlådan.**
> *I'm in a sticky situation as I was late to work and the manager was already there.*

Jag åt upp min systers påskägg så nu sitter jag med skägget i brevlådan.

I ate my sister's Easter egg, so now I'm in trouble.

Nu är det dags att öva! Look at the three situations described below. In which of these would the expression **sitter du med skägget i brevlådan** be appropriate? Once you've decided, circle the corresponding number or numbers.

1. Du går utklädd till monster på en Halloweenfest men ingen annan har klätt ut sig.
2. Du kallar någon som heter Lisa för Britta en hel dag.
3. Du går på bio med en kompis och har det jättetrevligt.

* * *

When you think you know the answers, turn to page 62 to check if you're right.

4

I KLASSRUMMET

SAY WHAT YOU SEE

What is happening in the picture below? In this activity you will practise your writing skills. Below is a list of suggested words and sentence starters to help you describe the scene. Use these to write three to five sentences about what you can see in the picture. **Lycka till!**

SUGGESTED WORDS AND PHRASES

på bilden ser man - in the picture you see
på höger sida - on the right-hand side
på vänster sida - on the left-hand side
i mitten - in the middle
i bakgrunden - in the background
(ett) klassrum - classroom
att stå - to stand
att sitta - to sit
(en) lärare - teacher
framför - in front of
tal (ett word) - numbers, sums
står skrivna - are written
att se glad ut - to look happy
att le - to smile
(en) skjorta - shirt
(en) kofta - cardigan
en bok i handen - a book in (her) hand
(en) anteckningsbok - notebook
att ha på sig - to wear
att peka på - to point at
(en) matematiklektion - maths lesson
elever (en word) - pupils
skolbarn (ett word) - school children
på svarta tavlan - on the blackboard
räcker upp händerna - raising their hands
bänkar (en word) - desks
böcker (en word) - books
har kort hår - has short hair
har långt, lockigt hår - has long, curly hair

I klassrummet

✎ _____

_____

_____

_____

_____

_____

_____

_____

_____

_____

_____

* * *

Strålande! Now you can have a look at the example answer on page 63.

ATT HA EN MORMOR
GUIDED TRANSLATION

In this Guided Translation we will take a look at a quote about unconditional love from the popular Swedish writer Fredrik Backman.

Att ha en mormor är som att ha en armé. Det är ett barns yttersta privilegium att veta att nån står på din sida. Till och med när du har fel, speciellt då faktiskt.
FREDRIK BACKMAN

Att ha en mormor är som att ha en armé. Det är ett barns yttersta privilegium att veta att nån står på din sida. Till och med när du har fel, speciellt då faktiskt.

FREDRIK BACKMAN

LANGUAGE EXPLANATION

In the first sentence of this quote, we have two phrases: **att ha en mormor** ("to have a maternal grandmother") and **att ha en armé** ("to have an army"). By putting **är som** ("is like") between the two phrases they are connected and form a simile.

The next part of the quote explains why it's so special for a child to have a grandmother.

As part of Backman's informal writing style, he uses the word **nån**, which is usually only used in spoken Swedish. It is a short form of **någon** ("somebody").

In the same sentence, we see the idiom **står på din sida** ("to be on your side"), which is used to describe somebody who supports you.

In the final sentence, Backman begins to explain how the support a grandmother gives to their grandchild is unconditional. He writes **till och med när** ("even when"), then **har fel**, which means "to be wrong". Notice how the verb **har** ("have") is used together with **fel** ("wrong") in Swedish, unlike in English where we use the verb "be".

Backman's use of adverbs and adjectives like **yttersta** ("utmost"), **speciellt** ("especially") and **faktiskt** ("actually") is very typical of his style and helps to create his engaging, informal tone that makes his books very accessible for learners who want to read books in Swedish.

Now, using all the information above, can you try translating this quote?

TRANSLATION:

✎ _____

_____

_____

_____

_____

* * *

Once you're happy with your answer, turn to page 63 to find a translation.

6

DJURNAMN
WORD BUILDER

You are probably familiar with the Swedish words **hund** ("dog") and **katt** ("cat"), as they are our most common **husdjur** ("pets"), but how many other animals do you know in Swedish? In this Word Builder we're going to learn some new animal words, which may come in handy if you are visiting **Skansen** in Stockholm or another Swedish **djurpark** ("zoo").

* * *

Most animals are **en** nouns, but you'll notice that a few animals in our list are **ett** nouns. Here are the names of some other common animals in Swedish:

(en) älg - moose
(en) björn - bear
(en) ekorre - squirrel
(en) apa - monkey
(ett) marsvin - guinea pig

(ett) får - sheep
(ett) bi - bee
(en) spindel - spider
(en) varg - wolf
(en) orm - snake
(en) anka - duck
(ett) lejon - lion

Vilket är ditt favoritdjur och varför? Let's put into practice some of this new vocabulary by answering the question: "what is your favourite animal and why?" Write a short paragraph below using these new animals or other vocabulary you already know. **Lycka till!**

✎_____

_____

_____

_____

_____

_____

_____

_____

_____

_____

_____

7

SAMMANSATTA ORD
MINI GRAMMAR CHALLENGE

This Mini Grammar Challenge is all about compound words. Some Swedish words can look intimidating to an English speaker because they are so long, but that's because Swedish uses more compound words than English. To see words like **biljettkontorspersonal** ("ticket office staff") or **bordsservering** ("table service") when you are on holiday might be daunting – but there's no need to worry! When you start looking at these long words and breaking them down, you'll see they're often not too different from their English translations. It's just that they are written as one word rather than two, or even three, words. Let's take a closer look at how to form compound words, then have a go at the exercises that follow. **Låt oss börja!**

* * *

Compound words are created by joining two or more words together. A compound word will always take the gender of the last word. If the first noun ends with a vowel, this vowel is often dropped in a compound word. For example:

ficka + lampa → ficklampa
pocket + lamp → torch

If the first word is long, an -s- is often added. For example:

blåbär + paj → blåbärspaj
blueberry + pie → blueberry pie

EXERCISE 1

Look at these simple compound words and separate them into the two original words.

1. en fikarast

   ✎ _____

2. en födelsedagstårta

   ✎ _____

3. en svensklärare

   ✎ _____

4. en julafton

   ✎ _____

5. en fotbollsplan

   ✎ _____

EXERCISE 2

However, there are many compound words that don't always make immediate sense to a Swedish learner. Take a look at the examples below. Put the pairs of words together to make a new word. Can you guess what the compound word means?

1. **barn** + **vagn** ("child" + "carriage")

   ✎ _____

   TRANSLATION:

   ✎ _____

2. **strumpa** + **byxor** ("sock" + "trousers")

   ✎ _____

   TRANSLATION:

   ✎ _____

3. **sjuk** + **hus** ("sick" + "house")

   ✎ _____

   TRANSLATION:

   ✎ _____

4. **sköld** + **padda** ("shield" + "toad")

   ✎ _____

   TRANSLATION:

   ✎ _____

5. **färg** + **glad** ("colour" + "happy")

✎_____

TRANSLATION:

✎_____

* * *

Bra! When you're ready, you can find the answers to both exercises on page 63.

8

ATT VARA INSNÖAD
IDIOMATICALLY SPEAKING

It may not surprise you to know that there are many idiomatic expressions in Swedish about ice and snow. One example is **att vara insnöad**, "to be snowed in". It can be used in a literal sense, when it's been snowing so much that you can't leave your house or car. But it can also carry a second, more figurative meaning: that you are extremely interested in something, to the point that you are totally absorbed in it and it is almost an obsession. The idea is that you have "snowed yourself in" on something, **du har snöat in dig på något.** Let's take a look at some examples. First of all, let's see **att vara insnöad** used in its more literal sense:

Vi var insnöade hela helgen.
We were snowed in all weekend.

Now let's see how the expression can be used figuratively:

Jag kan allt om björnar. Jag har totalt snöat in mig på dem.
I know everything about bears. I'm obsessed with them.

**Jag måste sluta snöa in mig på vikingatiden men det
är så intressant!**
*I have to stop being so fixated on the Viking age, but it's so
interesting!*

Nu är det din tur! Can you come up with a few of your own
examples? Use the lines below to write three of your own
sentences using the expression **att vara insnöad.**

✎ _____

_____

_____

_____

_____

_____

_____

_____

_____

_____

9

PÅ ETT KAFÉ

SAY WHAT YOU SEE

Have a look at this picture of a scene in a café. How would you describe it? Practise your writing skills by coming up with three to five sentences about what you can see, using the suggested words and phrases to help you. **Lycka till!**

SUGGESTED WORDS AND PHRASES

på bilden - in the picture
till höger - to the right
till vänster - to the left
i mitten - in the middle
i bakgrunden - in the background
kan du se - you can see
tre vänner - three friends
att fika - to have a coffee and cake with friends
(en) man - man
två kvinnor - two women
tre kaffekoppar - three coffee cups
han tar sig för pannan - he grabs his forehead
(ett) par glasögon - pair of glasses
(ett) skägg - beard
randig - stripy
(en) hatt - hat
(en) blomma - flower
(en) axel - shoulder
(en) kofta - cardigan
att skratta - to laugh
att le - to smile
har på sig - is wearing
urdruckna - finished
(en) surfplatta - tablet

---

* * *

Bra jobbat! If you'd like to see an example answer, turn to page 64.

10

DET FINNS INGET DÅLIGT VÄDER BARA DÅLIGA KLÄDER
GUIDED TRANSLATION

In this Guided Translation we'll be taking a close look at the language used in a well-known Swedish saying: **det finns inget dåligt väder bara dåliga kläder**. Read the explanation below, then put all the information together and see if you can figure out the meaning.

* * *

LANGUAGE EXPLANATION

The saying starts with **det finns**, which means "there is" or "there are", or literally "there exists".

We can see in the first statement that **väder** ("weather") is an **ett** noun, as **inget** and the adjective **dåligt** ("bad") both end with **-t.**

Inget means "none", "not any" or "no". It changes to **ingen**, **inget** or **inga**, depending on whether the noun it refers to is an **en** noun, an **ett** noun or is plural. Have a look at these examples:

> **Jag har ingen hund.**
> *I don't have a dog.*

> **Jag har inget barn.**
> *I don't have a child.*

> **Jag har inga pengar.**
> *I don't have any money.*

The adjective **dålig** ("bad") is used again in the second part of the sentence, but as we are speaking about **kläder** ("clothes"), the adjective gets a plural **-a** ending: **dåliga**.

The two statements are connected by the word **bara**, which means "only".

So, can you put this all together and come up with a translation of this saying?

TRANSLATION:

✎ _____

_____

_____

_____

* * *

Bra jobbat! If you want to check that you understood the saying fully, turn to page 65.

11

PARTIKELVERB
WORD BUILDER

You may have already noticed in your Swedish learning that Swedish uses many phrasal verbs. In this Word Builder we're going to expand our vocabulary by focusing on some of these **partikelverb.**

* * *

Phrasal verbs are made up of a verb and a particle (a preposition or an adverb). A very well-known phrasal verb that you'll probably recognise is **tycker om** ("to like"), but there are many others. Familiarise yourself with the list below, then practise using these verbs in the exercise that follows.

att hoppa över - to skip
att hälsa på - to visit
att koppla av - to relax
att gå på - to cost
att skjuta upp - to postpone, to delay, to put off

att känna igen - to recognise
att gå med på - to accept, to agree to
att slå på - to turn on, to switch on
att packa upp - to unpack
att hänga med - to come along

Now fill in the gap in each sentence below with the correct phrasal verb. Watch out for your verb conjugations!

1. Vill du ✎_____ mormor och morfar i helgen?

2. Jag ✎_____ lunchen idag, jag är inte hungrig.

3. Min granne ✎_____ att vattna mina blommor när jag är på semester.

4. Kan du ✎_____ TV:n? Jag vill se nyheterna.

5. Har du ✎_____ resväskan?

6. Vi ska bara ✎_____ på semestern.

7. Hela middagen ✎_____ 700 kronor.

8. Jag ✎_____ dig! Bor du i Örebro?

9. Vi måste ✎_____ födelsedagsmiddagen eftersom Frida är sjuk.

10. ✎_____ till Sverige nästa gång vi åker.

The trickiest thing with Swedish phrasal verbs is the intonation. Try saying the phrasal verbs out loud to yourself and remember to put the stress on the particle (preposition or adverb), rather than the verb.

* * *

Utmärkt! When you're happy with your answers, you can check them on page 65.

12

DE ELLER DEM?

MINI GRAMMAR CHALLENGE

In this Mini Grammar Challenge we're looking at the difference between subject and object pronouns. Read the short explanation, then test yourself with the exercise that follows. **Är du redo? Då kör vi!**

* * *

Let's take a clear example phrase to see how subject and object pronouns work:

Jag älskar dig.
I love you.

Jag is the subject that is doing something in this phrase – in this case, **älskar. Dig** is an object, the person on the receiving end of the verb – in this case, being loved. Do you remember the other object pronouns?

Jag älskar mig.
I love me.

Jag älskar oss.
I love us.

Jag älskar dig.
I love you (singular).

Jag älskar er.
I love you (plural).

Jag älskar honom.
I love him.

Jag älskar dem.
I love them.

Jag älskar henne.
I love her.

Jag älskar det.
I love it (**ett** pronoun).

Jag älskar den.
I love it (**en** pronoun).

However, if you declare your love out loud, watch out for some tricky pronunciation points. Remember that the object pronouns **mig** and **dig** are pronounced **mej** and **dej**. And the really tricky ones are **de** and **dem**. **De** is a subject pronoun (meaning "they"), while **dem** is an object pronoun (meaning "them"), but both **de** and **dem** are pronounced **dom**.

EXERCISE

Let's focus on **de** and **dem** and practise when to use subject and object pronouns. Fill in the gaps in the sentences below with either **de** or **dem**.

1. Vad tycker ✎_____ ?
2. Jag tycker om ✎_____ .

3. Vill ✎_____ ha kaffe?

4. ✎_____ är inte hemma.

5. Jag tror på ✎_____ .

6. Magnus såg ✎_____ igår.

7. Hon gav ✎_____ en present.

8. ✎_____ hälsade på oss i måndags.

9. ✎_____ ringde mig förra veckan.

10. ✎_____ visade ✎_____ vägen?

* * *

Jättebra! When you're ready, check your answers on page 66 to see if you got them right.

13

INGEN FARA PÅ TAKET
IDIOMATICALLY SPEAKING

Have you ever reassured somebody by saying "no danger on the roof"? Perhaps not in English, but in Swedish **ingen fara på taket** is an idiomatic expression that is used to tell somebody not to worry. Here's an example:

A: Jag glömde att boka bord!
B: Ingen fara på taket, det gjorde jag igår.

A: I forgot to book a table!
B: Don't worry, I did that yesterday.

This idiom can often be shortened to simply **ingen fara**.

Be careful, though. **Fara** can be both a verb and a noun: **att fara** means "to go" and **en fara** means "a danger", so it's important that we understand the context.

You may come across **fara** used as a verb in another idiomatic expression: **fara och flyga**. This phrase literally means "go and fly", and you could say it to somebody if you were annoyed with them and wanted them to leave. For example:

Han är så sur. Han kan fara och flyga!
He is so grumpy. He can get lost!

Låt oss öva! Look at the following scenarios and consider our two idiomatic expressions. In each situation, what would you say?

1. Din lillasyster är nervös för ett prov hon har imorgon.

    ✎ _____

2. Någon är otrevlig mot dig på gatan.

    ✎ _____

3. En man ber om ursäkt för han har ringt fel.

    ✎ _____

4. Ett bi landar på din glass.

    ✎ _____

* * *

Once you're happy with your answers, turn to page 67 to check them.

14

I SNÖN

SAY WHAT YOU SEE

In this activity you'll have the chance to practise your writing skills. Take a close look at the picture below and think about how you would describe what is happening in it. On the next page, there are some suggested words and phrases to help you write three to five sentences describing the scene. **Lycka till!**

SUGGESTED WORDS AND PHRASES

på bilden - in the picture
att göra en snögubbe - to make a snowman
snön ligger på marken - the snow is on the ground
(ett) par - couple
att le - to smile
stenar (en word) - stones
knappar (en word) - buttons
två pinnar - two sticks
armar (en word) - arms
att huka sig ner - to crouch down
(ett) skägg - beard
(en) tumvante - mitten
(en) täckjacka - winter jacket, quilted jacket
(en) mössa - woolly hat
långt, blont hår - long, blond hair
båda två - both of them
kängor (en word) - boots
(ett) par jeans - pair of jeans
(en) tröja - jumper, sweater
knuten runt halsen - tied around the neck
i bakgrunden - in the background
granar (en word) - fir trees

I snön

✏️ _____

_____

_____

_____

_____

_____

_____

_____

_____

_____

_____

* * *

Bra! When you're happy with your paragraph, you can have a look at page 68 for an example answer.

15

MAN SKA INTE PRATA OM SIN LYCKA
GUIDED TRANSLATION

This Guided Translation will take you through the language used in a quote from the famous Swedish writer and playwright August Strindberg. Read through the language explanation, then see if you can piece it all together and come up with a translation of the quote. **Låt oss börja!**

Man ska inte prata om sin lycka, olyckan kan stå och lyssna.

AUGUST STRINDBERG

LANGUAGE EXPLANATION

Strindberg speaks to a general "you" by starting the sentence with **man**. **Man** is a very common word used to speak about people in general in Swedish and can be translated by "one" or "you" in English.

The quote has two auxiliary verbs. One of them is **ska**, in the first part of the sentence. **Ska** means "should" here, but it is followed by **inte**. Strindberg is telling us that we "should not" do something.

The next verb, **prata**, is an infinitive, as it comes after an auxiliary verb. **Prata** is a verb we're sure you're very familiar with, for example from phrases such as **jag pratar svenska**.

In the next part of the sentence, another auxiliary verb is used: **kan**. This usually means "can", but in certain contexts it can be translated as "could". The two other verbs that follow are also infinitives: **stå** ("to stand") and **lyssna** ("to listen").

In the quote, Strindberg makes the stylistic choice of using the noun **lycka** ("fortune" or "happiness") in the first part of the sentence, before using its opposite, **olycka** ("misfortune" or "unhappiness") in the second part of the sentence.

Adding an **o-** to the start of a word is often how simple it can be to create opposite nouns and adjectives in Swedish. Here are some other examples:

tur - luck	**otur** - bad luck, misfortune
trevlig - pleasant	**otrevlig** - unpleasant, rude
trolig - believable	**otrolig** - unbelievable
ro - tranquillity	**oro** - unrest, anxiety, worry
van - used to, accustomed	**ovan** - unaccustomed
känd - known, famous	**okänd** - unknown
vänlig - friendly	**ovänlig** - unfriendly, disagreeable
artig - polite	**oartig** - impolite

With the information you have, try to translate the quote into English.

TRANSLATION:

✎_____

_____

_____

_____

* * *

When you're ready, turn to page 68 to check your answer.

16

DE FEM VACKRASTE ORDEN PÅ SVENSKA
WORD BUILDER

In 2015, the Swedish newspaper *Svenska Dagbladet* held a competition asking people to nominate the most beautiful words in Swedish. Let's see which five words their readers thought were the most beautiful in the Swedish language.

* * *

Take a look at the five words and see if you can match them with the definitions on the next page.

förgätmigej

snöflinga

porla

ögonblick

vemod

1. A word for a "moment", which can be translated literally as a "glance of an eye".

    ✎_____

2. A verb that describes the sound of a stream.

    ✎_____

3. Every single one of these is unique and they are made of frozen water falling from the sky.

    ✎_____

4. A word that does not have a precise translation but means roughly that you feel a tender sadness about something that is over.

    ✎_____

5. A small, blue flower that literally translates into the same name in English. Just like in English, it is one word made up of an old-fashioned phrase.

    ✎_____

* * *

When you think you know the answers, turn to page 68 to check them.

17

LÅNG ELLER KORT VOKAL?
MINI GRAMMAR CHALLENGE

You probably know by now from your language learning how important vowel sounds are in Swedish. In this Mini Grammar Challenge we're going to practise differentiating between pairs of words where the vowel alone creates a difference in meaning. Read the explanation below, then have a go at the exercise that follows. **Är du redo? Låt oss börja!**

* * *

Swedish vowels can be categorised as either "hard" vowels (**a, o, u** and **å**) or "soft" vowels (**e, i, y, ä** and **ö**). All vowels have a long and a short sound, but pay particular attention to **o**, which has two long sounds and two short sounds!

Luckily, when we read and write, there is a rule to help us remember whether we need to use a long or a short vowel: a long vowel is followed by a single consonant, while a short vowel is followed by two consonants.

But this means that small differences in spelling and pronunciation sometimes produce completely different words – even if the two words look and sound very similar! For example, it's easy to accidentally say or write **tak** ("roof") instead of **tack** ("thank you").

Have a look at the word pairs below. The words on the left have long vowel sounds and those on the right have short vowel sounds.

tak - ceiling, roof	**tack** - thank you
granen - the fir tree	**grannen** - the neighbour
mata - to feed	**matta** - rug
väg - road	**vägg** - wall
glas - glass	**glass** - ice cream
kola - fudge	**kolla** - to check
ful - ugly	**full** - drunk, full
kal - bare	**kall** - cold

Take some time and try to say these words out loud to yourself. Can you hear the difference?

EXERCISE

Complete the following sentences by circling the correct word from each pair.

1. **Tak / Tack** så jättemycket för middagen igår. Det var jättetrevligt!
2. Den nya **granen / grannen** verkar vara trevlig. Jag träffade honom igår.

3. Vilken fin **mata / matta** du har! Är den från IKEA?

4. **Glas / Glass** är min favoritdessert.

5. Jag vet inte var vi är, vi måste fråga om **vägen / väggen**.

6. Jag fryser och är **kal / kall**.

7. Vill du **mata / matta** hästarna?

8. Jag måste **kola / kolla** en sak.

9. Kan jag få ett **glas / glass** rött vin?

10. Vill du ha **kolasås / kollasås** på **glasen / glassen**?

* * *

Bra jobbat! When you're ready, you can check your answers on page 69.

18

ATT KASTA SAKER I SJÖN
IDIOMATICALLY SPEAKING

In this activity we have two interesting Swedish idioms for you, both of which involve throwing things in a lake! In both expressions, we're going to be using the verb **att kasta** ("to throw") and the phrase **i sjön** ("in the lake"), but the two idioms mean very different things. To throw **pengar** ("money") in the lake means "to waste money", while to throw **yxan** ("the axe") into the lake means "to give up". In English, we have two similar expressions, which also involve throwing things! **Att kasta pengar i sjön** is similar to "to throw money down the drain" and **att kasta yxan i sjön** could be compared to "to throw in the towel". Now, let's see some examples in context:

Det är att kasta pengarna i sjön att köpa den dyrare mobiltelefonen.

It's a waste of money to buy the more expensive mobile phone.

**Vi skulle aldrig ha gått till den där restaurangen.
Det var att kasta pengar i sjön.**
*We should never have gone to that restaurant. It was
money down the drain.*

**Jag trivdes inte på universitetet första året men jag
ville inte kasta yxan i sjön.**
*I didn't enjoy university the first year, but I didn't want to
give up.*

**Det är bara tre kilometer kvar på loppet. Du kan
inte kasta yxan i sjön nu.**
*There are only three kilometres left of the race. You can't
throw in the towel now.*

Nu är det din tur! Take a look at these scenarios. Which ones
are about **att kasta pengar** and which ones are about **att kasta
yxan?**

1. Anna har gett upp att lära sig spela gitarr.

   ✎ _____

2. Maria åkte på en dyr solsemester men det regnade hela
   veckan.

   ✎ _____

3. Erik har bestämt sig för att sluta vara skådespelare och
   studera till lärare istället.

   ✎ _____

4. Björn köpte en tröja för 2 000 kronor men den passade inte.

✎_____

* * *

Jättebra! When you're ready, turn to page 70 to check your answers.

19

I KÖKET

SAY WHAT YOU SEE

What's happening in the photo below? Practise your writing skills by coming up with a short descriptive paragraph about the scene. On the next page, you can find some helpful words and phrases. **Lycka till!**

SUGGESTED WORDS AND PHRASES

på bilden - in the picture
till vänster - to the left
till höger - to the right
i bakgrunden - in the background
tre vänner - three friends
(ett) kök - kitchen
de står vid köksbänken - they are standing by the kitchen counter
(en) kökshandduk - tea towel
(en) ostbit - piece of cheese
(en) skål - bowl
citroner (en word) - lemons
sparris (en word) - asparagus
en av kvinnorna - one of the women
(en) spis - hob
(en) man - man
två kvinnor - two women
brunhårig - brown-haired
han håller i stekpannan - he is holding a frying pan
tre vinglas - three wine glasses
han har en rutig skjorta på sig - he is wearing a checked shirt
hon har ett förkläde på sig - she is wearing an apron
de lagar mat tillsammans - they are cooking together
på hyllorna - on the shelves
solen skiner - the sun is shining
genom fönstret - through the window

_____

_____

_____

_____

_____

_____

_____

_____

_____

_____

_____

* * *

Utmärkt! If you'd like to see an example paragraph, turn to page 71.

20

EN GÖTEBORGSVITS
GUIDED TRANSLATION

Göteborg, Sweden's second largest city, is known for a particular type of humour called **göteborgsvitsar**. **En vits** is a joke that is a play on words, a pun, and the point of **en göteborgsvits** is that it is dry and simple. Trying to understand jokes in the language you're learning can be a good test of your language skills and cultural knowledge, so let's take a look at **en göteborgsvits** together and see if you can work out why it's funny!

* * *

Here's the joke:

A: **Ligger snön kvar länge på gatorna om det snöar i Edinburgh?**

B: **Nej, där bor över en halv miljon människor, alla skottar.**

Did you understand the **vits**?

LANGUAGE EXPLANATION

We'll start by translating the question. When asking a yes-or-no question in Swedish, you can turn a statement into a question simply by swapping the position of the verb and subject.

This question starts with the phrasal verb **ligga kvar**, which means "to remain lying". For example:

Jag ligger kvar i sängen.
I remain lying in bed / I'm still lying in bed.

In the joke, we see **ligga kvar** in the context of **snön ligger kvar på gatorna** ("the snow remains lying on the street / the snow is still lying on the street").

There are two similar words in the question: **snön** and **snöar**. **Snö** is simply the noun "snow" and, as it ends with a vowel, the definite form is created by adding **-n: snön** ("the snow").

Att snöa is a verb ("to snow") and to make it into present tense an **-r** is added at the end.

The word **om** means "if".

Now that we have worked out what the question is, let's have a look at the answer, as this is where the punchline is.

The pun here is that a Scottish person is called **en skotte** in Swedish. Like most nouns ending with **-e**, the plural ending is

-ar. So, the half a million Scottish people living in Edinburgh are all **skottar**.

However, **att skotta** is a verb, meaning "to shovel snow". The present tense of **skotta** is **skottar**, spelled the same way as the plural noun for Scottish people. So, we can also interpret the end of the joke as "all are shovelling snow".

Very often, jokes can't be translated word for word into another language, especially when they involve plays on words, but that's why they're a good test of your understanding!

Use the lines below to piece together the information above and write down your translation, even if the double meaning is lost in English.

TRANSLATION:

_____

_____

_____

_____

_____

* * *

Bra jobbat! When you think you've got it, have a look at our translation on page 71.

ANSWERS

5-MINUTE COFFEE BREAKS

VILKEN, VILKET ELLER VILKA?
Mini Grammar Challenge

1. Q: **Vilket** hus bor Tora i?

   A: Hon bor i det stora vita huset bredvid tågstationen.

   TRANSLATION:

   Q: *Which house does Tora live in?*

   A: *She lives in the big white house by the train station.*

2. Q: **Vilket** land kommer du ifrån?

   A: Jag kommer ifrån Norge.

   TRANSLATION:

   Q: *Which country do you come from?*

   A: *I come from Norway.*

3. Q: **Vilket** universitet går du på?

   A: Jag går på Uppsala universitet.

TRANSLATION:

Q: *Which university do you go to?*

A: *I go to Uppsala University.*

4. Q: **Vilka** språk talar du?

A: Jag talar både svenska och finska.

TRANSLATION:

Q: *Which languages do you speak?*

A: *I speak both Swedish and Finnish.*

5. Q: **Vilken** är din favoritfärg?

A: Min favoritfärg är röd.

TRANSLATION:

Q: *What is your favourite colour?*

A: *My favourite colour is red.*

EXERCISE 2

1. Vilken trevlig lägenhet!
   What a nice flat!

2. Vilket ljuvligt väder!
   What lovely weather!

3. Vilka fina blommor!
   What nice flowers!

4. Vilken fantastisk bok!
   What a fantastic book!

D. Tack, jag har nyss flyttat in i den.
   Thanks, I just moved into it.

E. Ja, inte ett moln på himlen!
   Yes, not a cloud in the sky!

A. Varsågod, du är väl inte allergisk?
   You're welcome. You're not allergic, are you?

B. Eller hur? Hon är min favoritförfattare.
   Isn't it? She is my favourite author.

5. Vilka söta hundar du har!
   What cute dogs you have!

C. Visst är de? De heter Ludde och Ronja.

They are, aren't they? They are called Ludde and Ronja.

ATT SITTA MED SKÄGGET I BREVLÅDAN
Idiomatically Speaking

This idiom would be appropriate in situations 1 and 2.

1. Du sitter med skägget i brevlådan.
   Du går utklädd till monster på en Halloweenfest men ingen annan har klätt ut sig.
   TRANSLATION: *You go dressed up as a monster to a Halloween party but nobody else is wearing fancy dress.*

2. Du sitter med skägget i brevlådan.
   Du kallar någon som heter Lisa för Britta en hel dag.
   TRANSLATION: *You call somebody Britta all day whose name is actually Lisa.*

3. Du sitter inte med skägget i brevlådan.
   Du går på bio med en kompis och har det jättetrevligt.
   TRANSLATION: *You go to the cinema with a friend and have a lovely time.*

I KLASSRUMMET
Say What You See

HERE'S WHAT WE CAME UP WITH:

På bilden står en lärare i ett klassrum. Hon håller i en anteckningsbok och pekar på en elev. Hon ser glad ut. Hon har på sig en vit skjorta och en kofta. Framför läraren sitter eleverna. Det är en matematiklektion. På den svarta tavlan står tal skrivna. Skolbarnen räcker upp händerna. Man kan se sex händer. Man kan se två bänkar. På bänkarna ligger böcker. En elev har långt, lockigt hår. En elev har kort hår.

ATT HA EN MORMOR
Guided Translation

TRANSLATION: "Having a grandmother is like having an army. It is a child's utmost privilege to know that somebody is on your side. Even when you are wrong. Actually, especially then."

SAMMANSATTA ORD
Mini Grammar Challenge

EXERCISE 1

1. **fika + rast (en fikarast** - coffee break)
2. **födelsedag + tårta (en födelsedagstårta** - birthday cake)
3. **svenska + lärare (en svensklärare** - Swedish teacher)

4. **jul + afton** (**en julafton** - Christmas Eve)
5. **fotboll + plan** (**en fotbollsplan** - football pitch)

EXERCISE 2

1. **en barnvagn** - pram
2. **strumpbyxor** - tights
3. **ett sjukhus** - hospital
4. **en sköldpadda** - turtle
5. **färgglad** - colourful

PÅ ETT KAFÉ
Say What You See

HERE'S WHAT WE CAME UP WITH:

På bilden kan man se tre vänner som fikar tillsammans. Det är en man och två kvinnor. De skrattar och är glada. Till vänster sitter mannen. Han har ett skägg och en hatt på sig. Han skrattar så mycket att han tar sig för pannan. Kvinnan i mitten av bilden har en randig tröja på sig. Hon tittar på den andra kvinnan. Kvinnan till höger har glasögon, en vit tröja och en kofta på sig. Hon skrattar och rör den andra kvinnans axel. På bordet står tre urdruckna kaffekoppar och en blomma. Det ligger en surfplatta på bordet. I bakgrunden är fönstret öppet och man ser gröna träd.

DET FINNS INGET DÅLIGT VÄDER
BARA DÅLIGA KLÄDER
Guided Translation

TRANSLATION: "There's no such thing as bad weather, only bad clothing."

The outdoors is generally very popular in Sweden, and many Swedes would recognise this saying as something they were told as children, by their parents or teachers, when they didn't want to go outside because it was raining or snowing. The saying rhymes in Swedish, and it suggests that as long as you are dressed properly you can be outside in any weather!

PARTIKELVERB
Word Builder

1. Vill du **hälsa på** mormor och morfar i helgen?
   TRANSLATION: *Do you want to visit (maternal) Grandma and Grandpa this weekend?*
2. Jag **hoppar över** lunchen idag, jag är inte hungrig.
   TRANSLATION: *I'm skipping lunch today, I'm not hungry.*
3. Min granne **gick med på** att vattna mina blommor när jag är på semester.
   TRANSLATION: *My neighbour agreed to water my flowers when I'm on holiday / vacation.*
4. Kan du **slå på** TV:n? Jag vill se nyheterna.
   TRANSLATION: *Can you turn on the TV? I want to watch the news.*
5. Har du **packat upp** resväskan?
   TRANSLATION: *Have you unpacked your suitcase?*

6. Vi ska bara **koppla av** på semestern.

    TRANSLATION: *We are just going to relax on holiday.*

7. Hela middagen **gick på** 700 kronor.

    TRANSLATION: *The whole dinner cost 700 kronor.*

8. Jag **känner igen** dig! Bor du i Örebro?

    TRANSLATION: *I recognise you! Do you live in Örebro?*

9. Vi måste **skjuta upp** födelsedagsmiddagen eftersom Frida är sjuk.

    TRANSLATION: *We have to postpone the birthday dinner because Frida is ill.*

10. **Häng med** till Sverige nästa gång vi åker.

    TRANSLATION: *Come with us to Sweden next time we go.*

DE ELLER DEM?
Mini Grammar Challenge

1. Vad tycker **de**?

    TRANSLATION: *What do they think?*

2. Jag tycker om **dem**.

    TRANSLATION: *I like them.*

3. Vill **de** ha kaffe?

    TRANSLATION: *Do they want coffee?*

4. **De** är inte hemma.

    TRANSLATION: *They are not at home.*

5. Jag tror på **dem**.

    TRANSLATION: *I believe them.*

6. Magnus såg **dem** igår.

    TRANSLATION: *Magnus saw them yesterday.*

7. Hon gav **dem** en present.

   TRANSLATION: *She gave them a present.*

8. **De** hälsade på oss i måndags.

   TRANSLATION: *They visited us last Monday.*

9. **De** ringde mig förra veckan.

   TRANSLATION: *They called me last week.*

10. **De** visade **dem** vägen.

    TRANSLATION: *They gave them directions.*

INGEN FARA PÅ TAKET
Idiomatically Speaking

1. Ingen fara (på taket).

   Din lillasyster är nervös för ett prov hon har imorgon.

   TRANSLATION: *Your little sister is nervous about an exam she has tomorrow.*

2. Far och flyg.

   Någon är otrevlig mot dig på gatan.

   TRANSLATION: *Somebody is rude to you on the street.*

3. Ingen fara (på taket).

   En man ber om ursäkt för han har ringt fel.

   TRANSLATION: *A man apologises for dialling the wrong number.*

4. Far och flyg.

   Ett bi landar på din glass.

   TRANSLATION: *A bee lands on your ice cream.*

I SNÖN
Say What You See

HERE'S WHAT WE CAME UP WITH:

På bilden är det vinter. Snön ligger på marken. Man ser ett par. De gör en snögubbe. De ler mot varandra. Mellan dem står snögubben. Snögubben ler också. Snögubben har en mössa och en tröja knuten runt halsen. Han har stenar som ögon och knappar. Till vänster hukar mannen sig ner. Mannen har ett skägg. Han har på sig en täckjacka och en mössa. Kvinnan har också en täckjacka på sig och håller i en tumvante. Hon har långt blont hår och en mössa på sig. Båda två har jeans och kängor på sig. I bakgrunden ser man granar. Granarna har snö på sig.

MAN SKA INTE PRATA OM SIN LYCKA
Guided Translation

TRANSLATION: "You should not speak about your good fortune. Misfortune could be standing there listening."

DE FEM VACKRASTE ORDEN PÅ SVENSKA
Word Builder

1. **ögonblick** - moment, instant, blink of an eye
2. **porla** - babble, murmur or gurgle (referring to the sound of water or a stream)
3. **snöflinga** - snowflake

4. **vemod** - melancholy, wistfulness
5. **förgätmigej** - forget-me-not

LÅNG ELLER KORT VOKAL?
Mini Grammar Challenge

1. **Tack** så jättemycket för middagen igår. Det var jättetrevligt!

   TRANSLATION: *Thanks for the dinner yesterday. It was really nice!*

2. Den nya **grannen** verkar vara trevlig. Jag träffade honom igår.

   TRANSLATION: *The new neighbour seems nice. I met him yesterday.*

3. Vilken fin **matta** du har! Är den från IKEA?

   TRANSLATION: *What a nice rug you've got! Is it from IKEA?*

4. **Glass** är min favoritdessert.

   TRANSLATION: *Ice cream is my favourite dessert.*

5. Jag vet inte var vi är, vi måste fråga om **vägen**.

   TRANSLATION: *I don't know where we are. We have to ask for directions.*

6. Jag fryser och är **kall**.

   TRANSLATION: *I'm freezing and I'm cold.*

7. Vill du **mata** hästarna?

   TRANSLATION: *Do you want to feed the horses?*

8. Jag måste **kolla** en sak.

   TRANSLATION: *I have to check something.*

9. Kan jag få ett **glas** rött vin?

   TRANSLATION: *Can I have a glass of red wine?*

10. Vill du ha **kolasås** på **glassen?**

TRANSLATION: *Would you like fudge sauce on the ice cream?*

ATT KASTA SAKER I SJÖN
Idiomatically Speaking

1. Hon har kastat yxan i sjön.
Anna har gett upp att lära sig spela gitarr.
TRANSLATION: *Anna has given up learning to play the guitar.*

2. Maria kastade pengar i sjön.
Maria åkte på en dyr solsemester men det regnade hela veckan.
TRANSLATION: *Maria went on an expensive beach holiday, but it rained the whole week.*

3. Erik har kastat yxan i sjön.
Erik har bestämt sig för att sluta vara skådespelare och studera till lärare istället.
TRANSLATION: *Erik has decided to stop being an actor and start studying to become a teacher.*

4. Björn kastade pengar i sjön.
Björn köpte en tröja för 2 000 kronor men den passade inte.
TRANSLATION: *Björn bought a jumper for 2000 kronor, but it didn't fit.*

I KÖKET
Say What You See

HERE'S WHAT WE CAME UP WITH:

På bilden är det tre vänner som lagar mat tillsammans i ett kök. Solen skiner genom fönstret. Vännerna står vid köksbänken och dricker vin. På köksbänken står en skål med citroner och tre vinglas. Det ligger en ostbit och en kökshandduk på bänken. På spisen står en stekpanna. Mannen står vid fönstret och håller i stekpannan. De två kvinnorna skrattar. Kvinnan till vänster är blond och kvinnan till höger är brunhårig. Den brunhåriga kvinnan har på sig ett förkläde. Hon vänder på sparrisen i stekpannan. Både mannen och den blonda kvinnan har rutiga skjortor på sig. I bakgrunden finns det hyllor. På hyllorna ligger det böcker.

EN GÖTEBORGSVITS
Guided Translation

TRANSLATION:

A: Does the snow stay on the streets for long if it snows in Edinburgh?

B: No, over half a million people live there, all Scots / all shovelling snow.

10-MINUTE COFFEE BREAKS

CHECKLIST
10-MINUTE COFFEE BREAKS

Translation Challenge

Famous Swedish Speakers

Jumbled Letters

Number Focus
❏ Personnummer - page 87
❏ Hur mycket kostar den? - page 104
❏ Viktiga datum - page 120
❏ När fyller Alva år? - page 137

Taste Bud Tantaliser
❏ Ostkaka - page 90
❏ Våfflor - page 106
❏ Kärleksmums - page 123
❏ Janssons frestelse - page 140

21

ÖVERSÄTTNINGSÖVNING 1
TRANSLATION CHALLENGE

In this activity we'll be translating some sentences from English into Swedish. Try to do it independently to start with, but if you need some help you can find a hint for each sentence on the next page. **Lycka till!**

* * *

1. This year, I want to go to Gotland on holiday.

    ✎ _____

    _____

    _____

2. The lesson usually starts at 10 o'clock.

    ✎ _____

    _____

    _____

3. What a nice shirt you're wearing!

✎ _____

   _____

   _____

4. Are you going to the cinema tonight?

✎ _____

   _____

   _____

5. I don't like spiders.

✎ _____

   _____

   _____

HINTS

If you need some help, you may find the following hints useful.

1. Sentence 1 is going to start with a time phrase, which will affect the word order. We can't use the verb **gå** in this context.
2. For sentence 2, remember that the equivalent of "usually" in Swedish is a verb.

3. In sentence 3, we'll be using a reflexive verb. Also remember that the word for "shirt" is an **en** word.

4. In sentence 4, try not to use a verb that predicts, as if the outcome is predetermined. Instead, use a verb that expresses an intention or a choice. Use the preposition **på**.

5. For sentence 5, remember that when you use **inte** with a phrasal verb with two words, **inte** goes between the two words.

* * *

Snyggt jobbat! Once you're happy with your answers, you can find our suggested translations and further explanations on page 144.

22

GRETA THUNBERG
FAMOUS SWEDISH SPEAKERS

In this activity you'll be practising your reading skills while learning about a famous Swedish speaker, climate activist Greta Thunberg. Use the vocabulary list to help you as you read the text. Then, answer the comprehension questions to test your understanding. If you'd like an extra challenge, try reading the text and answering the questions without using the vocabulary list. Remember it's always there if you need some help. **Lycka till!**

* * *

Den mest kända svensken just nu är även den yngsta och den mest politiska. Miljöaktivisten Greta Thunberg började strejka utanför den svenska riksdagen i augusti 2018. Hon var bara 15 år gammal då. Hon satt på gatan med en gul regnjacka på sig. Hon höll upp en skylt som sa: "Skolstrejk för klimatet".

Hon strejkade varje fredag och uppmanade andra skolbarn att göra samma sak. Många skolbarn över hela världen blev inspirerade. I november 2018 strejkade över 17 000 skolbarn i 24 olika länder.

Greta Thunberg föddes 2003 i Stockholm. Hennes pappa är en skådespelare. Hennes mamma är en känd operasångerska som var med i Eurovisionsfestivalen 2009. Innan strejken hade Greta övertalat sin familj att sluta flyga och leva mer hållbart. Men hon kände att det inte var nog. Hennes föräldrar var oroliga för henne när hon började strejka men såg att hon mådde bättre av att vara engagerad i klimatfrågan.

Sedan 2018 har Greta hållit tal på FN-möten och talat inför politiker och ledare i många länder. Greta har inte bara haft en stor påverkan på klimatfrågan, hon har också blivit en symbol för de ungas röst. Hon har blivit nominerad till flera priser för sitt arbete, bl a Nobels fredspris.

VOCABULARY
(en) miljö - environment
(en) riksdag - parliament
(en) regnjacka - raincoat
(en) skylt - sign
att uppmana - to urge
(en) skådespelare - actor
(en) operasångerska - (female) opera singer
att övertala - to persuade
hållbart - sustainably
att känna - to feel

nog - enough
oroliga - worried
(ett) tal - speech
engagerad - engaged
FN (Förenta Nationerna) - UN (United Nations)
(en) påverkan - impact
bl a (bland annat) - among others, including

COMPREHENSION QUESTIONS

Answer the questions in English.

1. Where did Greta Thunberg start her strike?

   ✎ _____

   _____

2. What does her mother work as?

   ✎ _____

   _____

3. What did Greta persuade her family to do?

   ✎ _____

   _____

4. Did her parents encourage her to protest?

   ✎ _____

   _____

5. Towards the end of the text, we read that Greta has become a symbol of something. What is it?

✎_____

_____

* * *

Once you're ready, turn to page 146 to check your answers.

23

ANAGRAM 1
JUMBLED LETTERS

Below, you'll find two definitions and two words whose letters are jumbled up. Your task is to unscramble the letters to find the words defined. If you need some help, turn to page 86 to find a hint. Once you've done that, see how many other Swedish words (of three letters or more) you can make using the letters. **Lycka till!**

* * *

I. DEFINITION: en fest svenskar har i augusti då de äter skaldjur.

RAKTIVKFÄS

_____   _____

_____   _____

_____   _____

_____   _____

_____   _____
_____   _____
_____   _____
_____   _____
_____   _____
_____   _____
_____   _____

2. DEFINITION: en av Sveriges viktigaste dagar. Svenskar dansar runt en majstång. Svenskar sjunger om små grodor.

MISTANOMFODRMA

_____   _____
_____   _____
_____   _____
_____   _____
_____   _____
_____   _____
_____   _____
_____   _____
_____   _____

HINTS

1. This is a compound word. The first part is an animal and the second is a word for a party.
2. The word you're looking for is the name of a Swedish national holiday in June when the longest day of the year is celebrated.

* * *

Once you have tried to solve the two anagrams, you can check your answers on page 147.

24

PERSONNUMMER
NUMBER FOCUS

How well do you know your double-digit numbers in Swedish? In this activity we're going to practise our numbers in Swedish using **personnummer**. But first, we'll learn a little more about these "identity numbers". **Är du redo? Då börjar vi!**

* * *

If you have ever spent time in Sweden, you may have noticed that all Swedish citizens have a **personnummer** (an "identity number") and it can be difficult to do certain things or access services if you don't have one. A **personnummer** is made up of a person's date of birth (given in the format yy-mm-dd) followed by four digits that indicate where they were born and their gender. These extra numbers are known as **de fyra sista siffrorna** ("the last four digits"). However, when you hear these digits (and the full **personnummer**) read aloud, they tend to be given in pairs or double digits. Let's practise recognising two-digit numbers in Swedish by writing out the following **personnummer** in digits.

1. STAFFAN
   nittiotvå-nollett-tjugoett-nollnio-tio

   ✎ _____

2. TOR
   sjutton-tolv-fjorton-sjuttioåtta-trettioett

   ✎ _____

3. MAGNUS
   åttiosex-nollfem-elva-tjugonio-femtiofem

   ✎ _____

4. PIA
   fyrtiofem-elva-trettio-sextionio-fyrtioåtta

   ✎ _____

5. ESKIL
   nollfyra-nollnio-tjugofyra-arton-fjorton

   ✎ _____

6. AXEL
   fjorton-nolltre-femton-nollåtta-arton

   ✎ _____

7. OLLE

sextioåtta-tio-tolv-åttiotre-sjuttiotvå

✎_____

8. JOHAN

sjuttiosju-nollfyra-sexton-sjuttioett-femtiofyra

✎_____

9. TURE

elva-nolltvå-tjugosju-trettiosex-tretton

✎_____

10. KARIN

trettionio-nollåtta-fjorton-sjutton-tjugotvå

✎_____

* * *

When you're happy with your answers, turn to page 148 to see
if you got them right.

25

OSTKAKA

TASTE BUD TANTALISER

In our Taste Bud Tantalisers we use a recipe as a reading text and work through an exercise based on the language used in it. In this activity we have a traditional Swedish recipe. While it will take you longer than 10 minutes to make **ostkaka**, we can study and understand the text in that time. Read through it, then complete the exercise below, putting the steps into the correct order. **Lycka till!**

* * *

Svensk ostkaka är ett väldigt gammalt recept från 1500-talet. Den äts traditionellt i Småland i sydöstra Sverige och ska serveras ljummen.

INGREDIENSER

- 4 ägg
- 2 msk socker

- ½ dl vetemjöl
- 500 g keso
- 3 dl vispgrädde
- 1 dl hackad mandel
- 2 hackade bittermandlar

Servera med:
- 2 dl hjortronsylt
- 2 dl vispgrädde

GÖR SÅ HÄR

1. Sätt ugnen på 175°C.
2. Vispa ihop ägg och socker.
3. Rör i resten av ingredienserna.
4. Häll i en smord ugnssäker form.
5. Grädda i mitten av ugnen 35–45 min.
6. Servera ostkakan ljummen med hjortronsylt och vispad grädde.

VOCABULARY
den äts - it is eaten
Småland - a Swedish county
sydöstra - south-east
ljummen - lukewarm
msk (en matsked) - tablespoon
(ett) vetemjöl - wheat flour
(en) keso - cottage cheese
(en) vispgrädde - whipped cream
att hacka - to chop

(en) mandel - almond
(en) bittermandel - bitter almond
(en) hjortronsylt - cloudberry jam
att vispa - to whisk
att röra - to mix
att hälla - to pour
att grädda - to bake

EXERCISE

Without referring back to the recipe, translate the instructions below into English and put them into the correct order.

a) Häll i en smord ugnssäker form.

   TRANSLATION:

   _____

   _____

b) Grädda i mitten av ugnen 35–45 min.

   TRANSLATION:

   _____

   _____

c) Servera ostkakan ljummen med hjortronsylt och vispad grädde.

   TRANSLATION:

   _____

   _____

d) Sätt ugnen på 175°C.

TRANSLATION:

✎_____

_____

e) Rör i resten av ingredienserna.

TRANSLATION:

✎_____

_____

f) Vispa ihop ägg och socker.

TRANSLATION:

✎_____

_____

ORDER OF STEPS:

✎_____

* * *

Toppen! When you're ready, you can turn to page 149 to check your answers.

26

ÖVERSÄTTNINGSÖVNING 2
TRANSLATION CHALLENGE

Translate the sentences below into Swedish. Have a go on your own first, then if you need some help, turn the page to find some hints. **Är du redo? Då börjar vi!**

* * *

1. I've been to Luleå three times.

   ✎_____

   _____

   _____

2. She has a turtle called Kalle.

   ✎_____

   _____

   _____

3. I think I'm ill and need to go home.

    🖉_____

    _____

    _____

4. The sun was shining and the sea was blue.

    🖉_____

    _____

    _____

5. My grandmother is turning 93 years old tomorrow.

    🖉_____

    _____

    _____

HINTS

If you need some help, you may find the following hints useful.

1. In sentence 1, use the perfect tense. Also remember to use a noun for time that you can count.
2. In sentence 2, you can use a short word meaning "it" or "he" as a connector.
3. In sentence 3, use a verb indicating that you are not sure.
4. In sentence 4, the verb meaning "was shining" is irregular and has a different vowel from the present tense. The word for "the sea" is an **ett** noun.

5. For sentence 5, remember that the expression we use in Swedish when someone has a birthday translates literally as "to fill the year".

* * *

Jättebra! When you're ready, turn to page 149 to find our suggested translations and further language explanations.

27

TOVE JANSSON
FAMOUS SWEDISH SPEAKERS

In this activity we're focusing on a text about the famous Finnish children's author Tove Jansson. You can read the text as many times as you like before answering the comprehension questions that follow. Remember to use the vocabulary list to help you, if you need it. **Trevlig läsning!**

* * *

Många tänker på Tove Jansson som finsk och det är hon. Hon är lika finsk som saltlakrits, bastu och karelska piroger men hon var svensktalande. Det finns en svensktalande minoritet i Finland som heter finlandssvenskar och den berömda författaren Tove Jansson och hennes familj var finlandssvenskar så de berömda Muminböckerna skrevs faktiskt först på svenska.

Tove Jansson föddes i Helsingfors 1914 och fast de bodde i en stor stad tillbringade familjen sommaren i skärgården. Tove älskade att bo i skärgården och många av hennes böcker handlar om öar. När hon blev rik köpte hon en alldeles egen ö i Åbos skärgård. Familjen Jansson var en konstnärsfamilj och Tove gick på konstskola i Stockholm. Innan hon skrev Muminböckerna arbetade hon som konstnär och illustratör och hon fortsatte att måla hela livet.

Tove skrev den första Muminboken 1945. Hon sa att Mumin var hennes alter-ego och Muminmamman är baserad på hennes egen mamma. Mumin publicerades först som serie i den brittiska dagstidningen Evening Standard på 50-talet. Böckerna om Mumintrollet, hans familj och vänner blev väldigt populära. Barn skrev brev till Tove från hela världen och hon försökte alltid besvara breven personligen. Nu är böckerna översatta till ungefär femtio språk.

Förutom Muminböckerna skrev Tove Jansson böcker för vuxna hela sitt liv och hon dog 2001. Om du åker till Finland kan du besöka Mumindalen i den lilla hamnstaden Nådendal.

VOCABULARY

(en) saltlakrits - salty liquorice

(en) bastu - sauna

karelska piroger (en word) - pirogues: a filled pasty or pie from the Karelia region between Finland and Russia

(en) skärgård - archipelago

rik - rich

alldeles egen - very own

(en) konstnär - artist
(en) konst - art
(en) illustratör - illustrator
att fortsätta - to continue
(en) serie - comic
hela världen - the whole world
att besvara - answer
personligen - personally
översatta - translated
ungefär - approximately

COMPREHENSION QUESTIONS

Answer the following questions in English.

1. What are you called if you live in Finland but speak Swedish as your mother tongue?

   ✎ _____

   _____

2. Where was Tove Jansson born?

   ✎ _____

   _____

3. In which country were the Moomin stories published as a comic strip for the first time?

   ✎ _____

   _____

4. How many languages have the Moomin books been translated into?

✎_____

_____

5. In which town in Finland is there a Moomin Valley you can visit?

✎_____

_____

* * *

Duktigt! Once you're happy with your answers, you can turn to page 151 to check them.

28

ANAGRAM 2
JUMBLED LETTERS

Take a look at the two anagrams below. Unscramble the letters to find two Swedish words corresponding to the definitions. While you are working out the main word, write down any other Swedish words you can find (of three or more letters). If you need some help unscrambling the anagrams, you can find hints on page 103. **Lycka till!**

* * *

I. DEFINITION: en buffé med många svenska rätter. De kan vara både kalla och varma.

R M G S B Ö D S Å R O

_____ _____

_____ _____

_____ _____

_____   _____
_____   _____
_____   _____
_____   _____
_____   _____
_____   _____
_____   _____
_____   _____

2. DEFINITION: ett hus som svenskar åker på semester till i juni, juli eller augusti.

ASAGMRSTUOM

_____   _____
_____   _____
_____   _____
_____   _____
_____   _____
_____   _____
_____   _____
_____   _____
_____   _____

HINTS

1. This word doesn't have a direct translation in English, but we sometimes borrow the Swedish word in the context of food or to refer to a wide variety of choices in another context.
2. This is the word for a second home that some people live in during the summer.

* * *

When you're ready, you can find the anagram solutions on page 152.

29

HUR MYCKET KOSTAR DEN?
NUMBER FOCUS

In this Number Focus we are practising numbers in the context of prices. Read how much each item costs and write out the price in words, in Swedish.

* * *

1. Datorn kostar 10 999 kr att köpa.

   ✎_____

2. Tröjan kostar 448 kr.

   ✎_____

3. Lösgodiset kostar 19,90 kr per kilo.

   ✎_____

4. Byxorna är billiga och kostar 327 kr.

   ✎_____

5. Halsbandet brukade kosta 1 295 kr men på rea kostar det bara 895 kr.

   ✎ _____

6. Taxiresan kostade 587 kr utan dricks.

   ✎ _____

7. Svenska kräftor kostar 850 kr per kilo.

   ✎ _____

8. Dagens lunch kostar 120 kr.

   ✎ _____

9. Biljetterna kostade 175 kr styck.

   ✎ _____

10. En kaffe med påtår kostar 35 kr.

   ✎ _____

* * *

When you're ready, turn to page 153 to check your answers.

30

VÅFFLOR

TASTE BUD TANTALISER

This activity is based on a recipe for Swedish waffles, or **våfflor**. Read through the recipe, then answer the comprehension questions that follow. Later, why not try following the recipe and making **våfflor** yourself, to help you to get to know all this new vocabulary?

* * *

Den 25 mars är det våffeldag i Sverige. Från början heter dagen "Vårfrudagen" och är en kristen högtid men eftersom "vårfru" låter som våfflor på svenska började svenskar äta våfflor för att fira. De flesta svenska hushåll har ett våffeljärn hemma och våfflor äts året runt. Svenska våfflor är tunnare än belgiska våfflor och det används ett speciellt järn som gör våfflorna hjärtformade. Man kan både göra matiga och söta våfflor.

RECEPT 10 VÅFFLOR

INGREDIENSER

- 100 g smör
- 4 dl vetemjöl
- 0,5 tsk salt
- 1 tsk bakpulver
- 5 dl mjölk
- 2 ägg

GÖR SÅ HÄR

1. Smält smöret i en kastrull.
2. Blanda ihop de torra ingredienserna i en stor skål.
3. Vispa i mjölken.
4. Lägg till ägg och det smälta smöret.
5. Hetta upp våffeljärnet.
6. Lägg i en klick smör på våffeljärnet och häll i smeten för den första våfflan.
7. Grädda våfflorna tills de får fin färg.
8. Servera våfflorna med sylt och glass.
9. Smaklig måltid!

VOCABULARY

Vårfrudagen - Feast of the Annunciation
(en) högtid - holiday
att fira - to celebrate
(ett) våffeljärn - waffle iron

hjärtformade - heart-shaped
matiga - savoury
(ett) smör - butter
(ett) vetemjöl - wheat flour
tsk (en tesked) - teaspoon
(ett) bakpulver - baking powder
(en) mjölk - milk
(en) kastrull - saucepan
torr - dry
att hetta upp - to warm up
att hälla i - to pour in
(en) smet - batter
att grädda - to cook, to bake

COMPREHENSION QUESTIONS

Answer the following questions in English.

1. What date is Waffle Day in Sweden?

    _____

    _____

2. What's the difference between Swedish and Belgian waffles?

    _____

    _____

3. What do you start with when you make waffles?

✎_____

_____

4. What do you serve waffles with?

✎_____

_____

5. What is the equivalent of "bon appétit" in Swedish?

✎_____

_____

* * *

Think you've got them all right? When you're ready, you can check your answers on page 155.

31

ÖVERSÄTTNINGSÖVNING 3
TRANSLATION CHALLENGE

In this activity we have five sentences for you to translate into Swedish. See if you can work them out without any help, but there is a hint for each sentence on the next page if you need them. **Lycka till!**

* * *

1. I think that you are beautiful and you have beautiful brown eyes.

   ✎_____

   _____

   _____

2. What did you eat for breakfast this morning?

_____

_____

_____

3. There are four apples in a bowl on the table.

_____

_____

_____

4. My two Danish friends live in Malmö.

_____

_____

_____

5. Have you ever eaten crayfish?

_____

_____

_____

HINTS

If you need some help, you may find the following hints useful.

1. In sentence 1, you need to use a verb giving a personal opinion. A person is an **en** word.
2. For sentence 2, remember that "to eat" is an irregular verb and there is a particular word for "this morning" in Swedish.
3. In sentence 3, you need to use both the prepositions **på** and **i**. "Apple" is an **ett** word in Swedish.
4. You'll need to adjust the words for "my" and "Danish" in sentence 4 because they refer to your "friends".
5. In sentence 5, remember to use the perfect tense.

* * *

When you've finished your translations, turn to page 155 to see how you've done.

32

ABBA

FAMOUS SWEDISH SPEAKERS

If you're a regular Coffee Break Swedish learner, then you won't be surprised by the topic of the following reading text! In this activity we're focusing on a text about ABBA. Use the vocabulary list to help you as you read it, then answer the comprehension questions that follow. We'd recommend writing down any words that are new to you in your own notes, to help you remember them. **Lycka till!**

* * *

Sverige har lyckats göra och exportera mycket musik för att vara ett litet land. Men inga svenska musiker är så kända som sjuttiotalsgruppen ABBA. Gruppen splittrades 1982 men deras musik har fortsatt att vara populär.

Gruppen har fyra medlemmar, två kvinnor och två män. Namnet ABBA är den första bokstaven i deras förnamn:

Agnetha, Björn, Benny och Anni-Frid. När de vann Eurovisionfestivalen i England med låten "Waterloo" 1974 blev de världskända.

De fyra medlemmarna var två par. Agnetha och Björn var tillsammans och Anni-Frid och Benny var gifta med varandra. När de två paren fick äktenskapsproblem splittrades gruppen. Deras sista skiva *The Visitors* kallas deras "skilsmässoskiva". Björn och Benny fortsatte att jobba tillsammans och har skrivit musik till flera musikaler. 1999 gjorde de en musikal med gamla ABBA låtar. Den hette *Mamma Mia* och blev väldigt populär. Den blev senare en film med skådespelaren Meryl Streep.

2021 gjorde ABBA en comeback och släppte en ny skiva. Men de vill inte uppträda längre. Istället har de skapat en show i London där det är avatarer som uppträder.

Några av ABBAs låtar finns både på svenska och engelska. Vill du öva din svenska, lyssna på de svenska versionerna och sjung med. Då övar du ditt uttal och lär dig nya ord samtidigt. Om du tycker om ABBAs musik finns det ett ABBA museum i Stockholm. Där kan du se deras studio och scenkostymer.

VOCABULARY

att lyckas - to succeed

musiker (en word) - musicians

att splittras - to split up

medlemmar (en word) - members

(ett) äktenskapsproblem - marital problem
(en) skiva - record
(en) skilsmässa - divorce
att släppa - to release
att uppträda - to perform
att skapa - to create
avatarer (en word) - avatars
versionerna (en word) - the versions
scenkostymer (en word) - stage costumes

COMPREHENSION QUESTIONS

Answer the following questions in English.

1. What does ABBA mean?

   _____

   _____

2. When did ABBA become world famous?

   _____

   _____

3. Why did the group split up?

   _____

   _____

4. How is their album *The Visitors* often described?

✎_____

_____

5. How has ABBA solved the problem of not wanting to perform any longer?

✎_____

_____

* * *

Fantastiskt! Once you're happy with your answers, you can check them on page 157.

33

ANAGRAM 3
JUMBLED LETTERS

In this activity your challenge is to work out which words are hiding in the jumbled letters. Once you have unscrambled the anagrams to find the words that fit the definitions, write down all the other Swedish words (of three or more letters) you can make using those letters. There are hints in English on page 119 if you need them. **Lycka till!**

* * *

I. DEFINITION: en fisk som är gammal och luktar illa men man äter den ändå.

SÖMUSMIRNTGR

✎ _____   _____

_____   _____

_____   _____

_____   _____

_____

2. DEFINITION: en person som arbetar på ett sjukhus.

JAKTSSKERUKÖS

HINTS

1. This word is the name of a fermented Swedish delicacy.
2. The word you're looking for is a compound word. The first part means "sick" and the second part is a noun based on the verb "to care" in Swedish.

* * *

Once you're finished, you can turn to page 157 to find the answers.

34

VIKTIGA DATUM
NUMBER FOCUS

In this activity we are practising dates and ordinal numbers while learning about some important Swedish events. Write down the following dates and years in numerical figures. **Nu börjar vi!**

* * *

We've done the first one as an example:

Björn Borg vann Wimbledon första gången den tjugofjärde juni nittonhundrasjuttiosex.
24 June 1976

1. Den svenska kronprinsessan fyller år den fjortonde juli.

✎ _____

2. Varje vår firar man Valborgsmässoafton den trettionde april.

   ✎_____

3. Författaren Astrid Lindgren föddes den fjortonde november nittonhundrasju i Småland.

   ✎_____

4. Man äter våfflor den tjugofemte mars eftersom det är våffeldagen.

   ✎_____

5. Kung Gustav Vasa dog tjugonionde september femtonhundrasextio i Stockholm.

   ✎_____

6. Lucia firas alltid den trettonde december.

   ✎_____

7. Sveriges nationaldag är den sjätte juni.

   ✎_____

8. Nobeldagen är den tionde december och firas i både Stockholm och Oslo.

   ✎_____

9. Kanelbullens dag firas den fjärde oktober varje år.

   ✎_____

10. Sverige har vunnit Eurovisionsfestivalen sju gånger;
    nittonhundrasjuttiofyra, nittonhundraåttiofyra,
    nittonhundranittioett, nittonhundranittionio,
    tvåtusentolv, tvåtusenfemton och tvåtusentjugotre.

✎_____

* * *

Vad duktig du är! You can find the answers on page 159.

35

KÄRLEKSMUMS
TASTE BUD TANTALISER

Reading recipes in the language you're learning is a great way to practise the imperative – the verb form that you use when you give orders. "Whisk the cream" and "knead the dough" are both examples of the imperative. Here is a recipe for a popular Swedish chocolate traybake. Use the vocabulary list to help you as you read through it, then complete the exercise below to practise imperative verbs. **Ska vi sätta igång?**

* * *

RECEPT 16 KÄRLEKSMUMS

INGREDIENSER

- 200 g smör
- 2 dl mjölk
- 4 ägg
- 4 dl socker

- 4 dl vetemjöl
- 2 tsk vaniljsocker
- 1 ½ dl kakao
- 2 ½ tsk bakpulver
- 2 krm salt

Glasyr:
- 100 g smör
- ½ dl starkt kaffe
- 4 msk kakao
- 2 tsk vaniljsocker
- 5 dl florsocker

Garnering:
- 1 dl kokosflingor

GÖR SÅ HÄR

1. Sätt ugnen på 175°C.
2. Lägg bakplåtspapper i en form.
3. Smält smöret, häll i mjölken och låt det svalna.
4. Vispa ägg och socker riktigt pösigt med elvisp.
5. Blanda vetemjöl, vaniljsocker, kakao, bakpulver och salt.
6. Tillsätt smör och mjölk och blanda allt till en jämn smet. Häll smeten i formen.
7. Grädda kakan i mitten av ugnen i 25 minuter. Låt kakan svalna.

Glasyr:

8. Smält smöret i en kastrull och ta det från värmen.
   Tillsätt övriga ingredienser och rör till en jämn smet.
9. Bred glasyren över den avsvalnade kakan och strö över
   kokosflingorna.
10. Ställ kakan kallt tills glasyren stelnat. Skär
    kärleksmumsen i bitar.

VOCABULARY

(en) kärlek - love

mums - yummy

(ett) socker - sugar

(ett) vetemjöl - wheat flour

tsk (en tesked) - teaspoon

(ett) vaniljsocker - vanilla sugar

(en) kakao - cocoa powder

(ett) bakpulver - baking powder

krm (ett kryddmått) - literally "spice measure", about ¼ teaspoon

(en) glasyr - glaze

(ett) florsocker - icing sugar

(en) garnering - decoration

(ett) bakplåtspapper - baking paper

att hälla i - to pour in

(en) form - tin

pösigt - frothy

(en) elvisp - electric whisk

(en) smet - batter, mix

att grädda - to bake

att svalna - to cool down

att tillsätta - to add
att bre - to spread
att strö - to sprinkle

THE IMPERATIVE

If we know the imperative form of a verb, we can work out the verb's present tense ending.

If a verb ends in an **-a** in the imperative, it ends with **-ar** in the present tense. For example:

vispa > **vispar**
whisk (imperative) > *whisk(s)* (present)

If a verb ends with a consonant in the imperative, it ends with **-er** in the present tense. For example:

sätt > **sätter**
put (imperative) > *put(s)* (present)

If an imperative verb ends with any vowel other than **-a**, its present tense form simply ends with an **-r**. For example:

strö > **strör**
sprinkle (imperative) > *sprinkle(s)* (present)

There are also some irregular verbs to watch out for. Here are some examples:

gör > **gör**
do (imperative) > *do(es)* (present)

skär > **skär**
cut (imperative) > *cut(s)* (present)

EXERCISE

Read through the recipe again below. This time, we've left a gap where each of the verbs should be. Imagine you are making **kärleksmums** and you are describing what you are doing as you bake. Fill in the gaps using the verbs from the recipe, but this time in the present tense. We've done the first one for you.

1. **Jag sätter** ugnen på 175°C.

2. ✎_____ bakplåtspapper i en form.

3. ✎_____ smöret,
   ✎_____ i mjölken och
   ✎_____ det svalna.

4. ✎_____ ägg och socker riktigt pösigt med elvisp.

5. ✎_____ vetemjöl, vaniljsocker, kakao, bakpulver och salt.

6. ✎_____ smör och mjölk och
   ✎_____ allt till en jämn smet.
   ✎_____ smeten i formen.

7. ✎_____ kakan i mitten av ugnen i 25 minuter. ✎_____ kakan svalna.

8. ✎_____ smöret i en kastrull och
   ✎_____ det från värmen.
   ✎_____ övriga ingredienser och
   ✎_____ till en jämn smet.

9. 𖩹_____ glasyren över den
avsvalnade kakan och 𖩹_____ över
kokosflingorna.

10. 𖩹_____ kakan kallt tills glasyren
stelnat.

𖩹_____ kärleksmumsen i bitar.

* * *

Bra! When you're ready to check your answers, turn to
page 160.

36

ÖVERSÄTTNINGSÖVNING 4
TRANSLATION CHALLENGE

In this activity you'll be practising your translation skills by translating some sentences from English into Swedish. Have a go on your own first, but if you need some help you can turn the page to find a hint for each sentence.

* * *

1. How do you spell his surname?

   ✎ _____

   _____

   _____

2. Karlstad is in western Sweden.

   ✎ _____

   _____

   _____

3. The birds sing so beautifully in the spring.

✎_____

_____

_____

4. Have you got engaged? Congratulations!

✎_____

_____

_____

5. This summer, I went to Sweden on holiday.

✎_____

_____

_____

HINTS

If you need some help, you may find the following hints useful.

1. In sentence 1, the verb can be either passive or active.
2. In sentence 2, the verb **är** can't be used – you need to use a different verb.
3. For sentence 3, remember that "beautifully" is an adverb and a different preposition is used in Swedish from in English.
4. In sentence 4, you need to use a reflexive pronoun.
5. Pay attention to your sentence structure in sentence 5.

* * *

Kanon! When you're ready, check your answers on page 160.

37

ALFRED NOBEL

FAMOUS SWEDISH SPEAKERS

In this activity you will practise your reading skills while learning a little about Alfred Nobel, the founder of the Nobel Prize. Use the vocabulary list to help you as you read through the text, then answer the comprehension questions on the next page to test your understanding. If you'd like an extra challenge, why not try reading the text and answering the questions before looking at the vocabulary list? Remember it's always there if you need it. **Lycka till!**

* * *

Nobelpriset är ett av världens mest prestigefyllda pris. Men vem var Alfred Nobel? Jo, han var en man som levde på 1800-talet och uppfann dynamiten.

Alfred föddes 1833 i Stockholm men bodde som barn i Ryssland. Under sitt liv bodde han i många olika länder. Han talade svenska, ryska, engelska, franska, tyska och italienska flytande. Alfred utbildade sig till kemist. Han uppfann många saker och var en duktig affärsman. Han hade 90 företag i 20 olika länder och blev väldigt rik.

Alfred Nobel gifte sig aldrig och hade inga barn. Ett år innan han dog skrev han sitt testamente. Han skrev att hans pengar skulle delas upp i fem delar. Varje år skulle pengar ges till personer som förbättrar världen genom litteratur, kemi, medicin, fysik och fred.

Nobel dog i Italien 1896 och är begravd i Stockholm. Sedan 1901 delar man ut Nobelpriset varje år på Alfred Nobels dödsdag den 10 december. Dagen kallas Nobeldagen i Sverige och är en flaggdag. På Stortorget i Gamla stan i Stockholm finns det ett Nobelmuseum. Du kan besöka museet och lära dig mer om Nobelpriset och Alfred Nobel.

VOCABULARY

prestigefyllda - prestigious

att uppfinna - to invent

(en) dynamit - dynamite

flytande - fluent, fluently

att utbilda sig - to be educated, to be trained

(en) kemist - chemist

duktig - clever, able

(en) affärsman - businessman

(ett) företag - business, company

(ett) testamente - will

att förbättra - to improve

(en) fred - peace

begravd - buried

(en) flaggdag - flag day (a day when the Swedish flag is flown)

COMPREHENSION QUESTIONS

Answer the following questions in English.

1. Which languages did Alfred Nobel speak fluently?

   ✎_____

   _____

2. What kinds of people did Nobel want the prize to go to?

   ✎_____

   _____

3. When was the first Nobel Prize awarded?

   ✎_____

   _____

4. Why is Nobel Day on 10 December?

   ✎_____

   _____

5. Where is the Nobel Prize Museum?

   ✎_____

   _____

* * *

Once you're happy with your answers, turn to page 163 to check them.

38

ANAGRAM 4
JUMBLED LETTERS

Unscramble the letters of the two anagrams to find the words that correspond to the definitions. If you need some help, you can read the hints on page 136. Then, see how many other Swedish words (of three or more letters) you can make using the letters from the anagrams.

* * *

I. DEFINITION: man kan äta den när man fikar. Det är inte en kaka eller en tårta.

L E N L A L B E K U

_____   _____
_____   _____
_____   _____
_____   _____
_____   _____
_____   _____
_____   _____

2. DEFINITION: det är sött och rött. Svenskar äter det med köttbullar och potatismos.

NYTNSLGLOI

_____   _____
_____   _____
_____   _____
_____   _____
_____   _____
_____   _____
_____   _____
_____   _____
_____   _____

HINTS

1. This is the name of a Swedish sweet bun.
2. The word you're looking for is the name of a sweet sauce made from a Swedish berry.

* * *

Have you solved the anagrams? **Bra jobbat!** When you're ready, turn to page 163 to find the answers.

39

NÄR FYLLER ALVA ÅR?

NUMBER FOCUS

In this activity we're going to read a text about Alva which is full of numbers! Read the text as many times as you need to, then have a go at the two exercises that follow. **Tre, två, ett ... Nu kör vi!**

* * *

Alva bor på Kullagatan sjuttiotre. Lägenheten är en fyra och den ligger på första våningen. Hon har bott där i arton år. Alva fyller tjugo år i år. Hon fyller år den elfte juni. Alva bor där med sina föräldrar och två syskon. Hon är det andra barnet i syskonskaran. Hon har en storasyster och en lillebror. Hennes syster är tjugotvå år gammal och hennes bror är fjorton.

Alvas mormor och morfar bor också på Kullagatan men i nummer sextioåtta. De bor i en trea på fjärde våningen. Imorgon fyller Alvas morfar sjuttiofem år.

De ska ha en stor fest. Sextio släktingar och vänner är bjudna. Alva har femton kusiner och alla ska komma. Festen börjar klockan halv två. Alva ska vara där redan klockan elva och hjälpa till med maten. Alva ser fram emot festen. Det kommer att bli jättekul!

EXERCISE 1 - FIND THE NUMBERS

Answer the following questions, writing the numbers as numerical figures.

1. Which number does Alva live at?

   ✎ _____

2. When is Alva's birthday?

   ✎ _____

3. How old are Alva's siblings?

   ✎ _____

4. On which floor do Alva's grandparents live?

   ✎ _____

5. When does the party start?

   ✎ _____

EXERCISE 2 - OVER TO YOU

Write an answer in Swedish to each of these questions. Try to write the numbers in words.

1. När fyller du år?

_____

_____

2. Hur många syskon har du?

_____

_____

3. Hur gammal är du?

_____

_____

4. Vilket husnummer bor du på?

_____

_____

* * *

When you're finished, you can check your answers to Exercise 1 on page 165.

40

JANSSONS FRESTELSE
TASTE BUD TANTALISER

In this activity we're taking a look at a recipe for a delicious traditional fish and potato dish, **Janssons frestelse**. In some of the steps in the instructions, the prepositions **i** ("in") and **på** ("on") are missing. As you read the recipe, fill in each gap with the correct preposition. Then, answer the comprehension questions that follow. When you have more time, why not try making **Janssons frestelse**, following this recipe and getting to know the language in it better? **Lycka till med matlagningen!**

* * *

Janssons frestelse är en traditionell svensk rätt som svenskar oftast äter på julen, påsken eller på ett smörgåsbord.

Svenskar har ätit rätten i nästan 100 år. Janssons frestelse betyder "Jansson's temptation" och har fått sitt namn efter en film eller en operasångare men ingen vet säkert.

INGREDIENSER

- 3 stora gula lökar
- 1 ½ kg fast potatis
- 2 msk smör
- 3 burkar ansjovisfiléer (à 100 g)
- 4 dl vispgrädde
- 2 dl mjölk
- 2 msk ströbröd
- 3 msk smör eller margarin

GÖR SÅ HÄR

1. Sätt ugnen ✎_____ 200°C.
2. Skala och skär löken ✎_____ tunna skivor.
3. Fräs den mjuk ✎_____ lite smör ✎_____ en stekpanna.
4. Skala potatisen och skär den ✎_____ tunna strimlor.
5. Smörj en ugnssäker form.
6. Lägg ✎_____ ett lager potatis, därefter lök, ansjovis och sedan resten av potatisen. Häll ✎_____ grädde och mjölk. Strö över ströbrödet.
7. Grädda din Jansson ✎_____ nedre delen av ugnen 45–50 minuter.
8. Smaklig måltid!

VOCABULARY

(en) påsk - Easter
(en) rätt - dish
(en) operasångare - opera singer
säkert - for sure
(en) burk - tin
(en) ansjovis - anchovy
fast potatis (en word) - firm potatoes
(en) vispgrädde - double / heavy cream
(ett) ströbröd - breadcrumbs
att skala - to peel
att skära - to cut
att fräsa - to fry
(en) stekpanna - frying pan
att smörja - to grease
ungsäker - ovenproof
(en) tunn skiv - thin slice
strimlor (en word) - matchstick shapes, strips
(ett) lager - layer
därefter - then
att grädda - to bake, to cook
nedre - lower

COMPREHENSION QUESTIONS

Answer the following questions in English.

1. When do Swedes eat **Janssons frestelse?**

   ✎_____

   _____

2. Translate **frestelse** into English.

   ✎＿＿＿＿＿＿＿＿＿＿＿＿＿＿＿＿＿＿＿＿＿＿

   ＿＿＿＿＿＿＿＿＿＿＿＿＿＿＿＿＿＿＿＿＿＿＿

3. What do you do after chopping the onion?

   ✎＿＿＿＿＿＿＿＿＿＿＿＿＿＿＿＿＿＿＿＿＿＿

   ＿＿＿＿＿＿＿＿＿＿＿＿＿＿＿＿＿＿＿＿＿＿＿

4. What do you top the **Janssons frestelse** with?

   ✎＿＿＿＿＿＿＿＿＿＿＿＿＿＿＿＿＿＿＿＿＿＿

   ＿＿＿＿＿＿＿＿＿＿＿＿＿＿＿＿＿＿＿＿＿＿＿

5. In which part of the oven do you cook the dish?

   ✎＿＿＿＿＿＿＿＿＿＿＿＿＿＿＿＿＿＿＿＿＿＿

   ＿＿＿＿＿＿＿＿＿＿＿＿＿＿＿＿＿＿＿＿＿＿＿

* * *

Bra jobbat! Now you have completed both exercises, you can check your answers on page 165.

ANSWERS

ÖVERSÄTTNINGSÖVNING 1
Translation Challenge

1. I år vill jag åka till Gotland på semester.

EXPLANATION:

- As the sentence starts with a time phrase, the verb and subject change position.
- When it comes to travel, we always use the verb **åka**. If you use the verb **gå**, it sounds like you want to walk to your destination (and as Gotland is an island, that's definitely not a good idea!).

2. Lektionen brukar börja klockan 10.

EXPLANATION:

- While "usually" is an adverb in English, the Swedish equivalent, **brukar**, is an auxiliary verb. **Brukar** can't create a sentence by itself. This means that we need a second verb in the sentence, which is an infinitive.

- In Swedish, when telling the time, you always refer to "the clock" (**klockan**) and never "time" (**tid**).

3. Vilken snygg / fin skjorta du har på dig! /
   Vad snygg / fin skjorta du har på dig!

EXPLANATION:

- The word **vilken** could be used here in written or spoken Swedish. **Vad** is an alternative that can be used in spoken Swedish.
- **Vilken** takes the **en** form because **skjorta** is an **en** noun.
- **Att ha på sig** is both a phrasal and a reflexive verb. Because it is reflexive, you always have to include "on myself", "on herself" and so on. Here, we'd say "on yourself", so it would be **på dig**.

4. Ska / Tänker du gå på bio ikväll?

EXPLANATION:

- The verb **tänker** conveys less certainty – "are you planning to go to the cinema?" – while **ska** can be translated as a more certain "shall".
- You may wonder why we can't just translate this as **går du på bio ikväll?** While this would be a literal translation of "are you going to the cinema tonight?", it's more natural in Swedish to use the construction **ska du gå** or **tänker du gå** in this case. There's more information about this use of **tänka** in Activity 45 "Tycka, tro och tänka".

- The phrase **gå på bio** refers to the activity of attending the cinema in order to see a film. If you wrote **gå till bion**, this has a slightly different meaning – it sounds like you're asking if the person is going to walk to the cinema building.

5. Jag tycker inte om spindlar. / Jag gillar inte spindlar.

EXPLANATION:

- As **tycker om** is a phrasal verb consisting of two words, we need to put **inte** between **tycker** and **om**.
- If we choose the verb **gillar** instead, it is easier to make the sentence negative, as we simply put **inte** after it.
- **Spindel** is an **en** noun. When forming the plural, we want to avoid having two vowel sounds next to each other, so we drop the -**e**- and add the most common **en**-form plural ending, so that it becomes **spindlar**.

GRETA THUNBERG
Famous Swedish Speakers

1. Outside the Swedish parliament in Stockholm.
2. An opera singer.
3. To stop flying and live more sustainably.
4. No, they were worried about her doing it.
5. The voice of young people.

ANAGRAM 1
Jumbled Letters

1. **(en) kräftskiva** - crayfish party

   While there are many words that can be made out of these letters, here are some of the most common ones:

   - **(ett) fat** - large plate
   - **rik** - rich
   - **fria** - to propose
   - **(en) räka** - shrimp, prawn
   - **(en) vikt** - weight
   - **fikar** - having a coffee and a cake with friends
   - **frisk** - healthy
   - **färsk** - fresh
   - **(en) avsikt** - intention
   - **fiskar** - fish (plural)
   - **skrika** - to scream
   - **(en) trafik** - traffic
   - **(en) vätska** - fluid

2. **(en) Midsommarafton** - Midsummer's Eve
   - **(en) fot** - foot
   - **fri** - free
   - **roa** - to entertain
   - **(en) tid** - time
   - **(ett) foto** - photo
   - **(en) dator** - computer
   - **(en) dimma** - fog
   - **simma** - to swim

- **inrama** - to frame
- **timmar** - hours
- **(en) anatomi** - anatomy
- **(en) diamant** - diamond
- **(en) fantasi** - imagination
- **(en) framtid** - future
- **omfamna** - to embrace
- **(en) framsida** - front page
- **(en) sommartid** - summertime

PERSONNUMMER
Number Focus

1. STAFFAN
   92-01-21-09-10
2. TOR
   17-12-14-78-31
3. MAGNUS
   86-05-11-29-55
4. PIA
   45-11-30-69-48
5. ESKIL
   04-09-24-18-14
6. AXEL
   14-03-15-08-18
7. OLLE
   68-10-12-83-72
8. JOHAN
   77-04-16-71-54

9. TURE

   11-02-27-36-13

10. KARIN

    39-08-14-17-22

OSTKAKA
Taste Bud Tantaliser

a) Pour into a greased ovenproof dish.

b) Bake in the middle of the oven for 35–45 minutes.

c) Serve the cheesecake lukewarm with cloudberry jam and whipped cream.

d) Set the oven to 175°C.

e) Mix in the rest of the ingredients.

f) Whisk together eggs and sugar.

ORDER OF STEPS: d), f), e), a), b), c)

ÖVERSÄTTNINGSÖVNING 2
Translation Challenge

1. Jag har varit i Luleå tre gånger.

EXPLANATION:

- Just like in English, we use the perfect tense when speaking about whether or not something has happened (rather than the simple past tense to say when it happened, as in **jag var i Luleå 2010** - "I was in Luleå in 2010").

- When we speak about how many times something has happened, we use the time noun **gång**: for example **en gång**, **två gånger**, **tre gånger**.

2. Hon har en sköldpadda som heter Kalle. / Hon har en sköldpadda. Den heter Kalle.

EXPLANATION:

- Both of these translations are correct and, whichever you choose, a pronoun is required.
- One option is to split it into two sentences and start the second sentence with the pronoun **den: den heter Kalle** ("it's called Kalle").
- We can also use **som**, which is the equivalent of "who" (or "that" or "which") in English. Here, it can be used as a connector and a pronoun, allowing you to say the same thing in one longer sentence.

3. Jag tror att jag är sjuk och behöver gå hem.

EXPLANATION:

- If you're not certain of something, the verb **tror** is used, rather than **tycker** or **tänker. Tycker** is used to give a personal opinion, while **tänker** is used to talk about what you are thinking about or planning to do. In this context, we'd therefore translate "think" using **tror**.
- Notice that we end the sentence with **hem** rather than **hemma**, as **hem** is used when we are talking about home as a direction or destination. When we are *at* home, we say **hemma**.

4. Solen sken och havet var blått.

EXPLANATION:

- **Solen skiner** in the present tense becomes **solen sken** in the past tense.
- As **hav** ("sea") is an **ett** word, "the sea" is **havet**. When describing it as "blue", the correct form of the adjective **blå** is **blått**.

5. Min mormor / farmor fyller 93 år imorgon.

EXPLANATION:

- In Swedish, most relatives are divided into the maternal or paternal sides. Therefore, "grandmother" can be translated as either **farmor** ("paternal grandmother") or **mormor** ("maternal grandmother").
- We use the verb **att fylla**, "to fill (the year)", when speaking about having a birthday.

TOVE JANSSON
Famous Swedish Speakers

1. **Finlandssvensk** (literally, "Finland Swedish").
2. Helsinki (which is called **Helsingfors** in Swedish).
3. The UK.
4. Approximately 50 languages.
5. **Nådendal,** a small seaside town outside Turku (which is called **Åbo** in Swedish). The town is called Naantali in Finnish and English.

ANAGRAM 2
Jumbled Letters

1. **(ett) smörgåsbord**

   Here are some of the common words that can be made out of these letters:

   - **(en) gås** - goose
   - **(en) mor** - mother
   - **(ett) råd** - advice
   - **små** - small
   - **(en) sås** - sauce
   - **(ett) bord** - table
   - **(en) borg** - fort
   - **(en) bror** - brother
   - **(ett) bröd** - bread
   - **(en) dröm** - dream
   - **(en) dörr** - door
   - **möss** - mice
   - **öbor** - islanders
   - **orörd** - untouched
   - **smord** - greased
   - **bördor** - burdens
   - **grödor** - crops
   - **mössor** - woolly hats
   - **omrörs** - stirred
   - **(en) smörgås** - sandwich

2. **(en) sommarstuga** - summer cottage
   - **arg** - angry
   - **(en) otur** - bad luck

- **(en) ruta** - box, square
- **stor** - large
- **surt** - sour
- **(ett) torg** - town square
- **gasar** - accelerating
- **gator** - streets
- **osagt** - unsaid
- **osams** - at odds
- **sagor** - fairy tales
- **stora** - large (plural)
- **(en) storm** - storm
- **gummor** - old women
- **somras** - last summer
- **(ett) tomrum** - void
- **tummar** - thumbs
- **smutsar** - soiling
- **stammar** - stuttering
- **tursamma** - lucky

HUR MYCKET KOSTAR DEN?
Number Focus

1. **tiotusenniohundranittionio kronor**
   Datorn kostar 10 999 kr att köpa.
   TRANSLATION: *The computer costs 10,999 kr to buy.*
2. **fyrahundrafyrtioåtta kronor**
   Tröjan kostar 448 kr.
   TRANSLATION: *The jumper / sweater costs 448 kr.*

3. **nitton kronor och nittio öre**
   Lösgodiset kostar 19,90 kr per kilo.
   TRANSLATION: *The pick 'n' mix / loose candy costs 19.90 kr per kilo.*

4. **trehundratjugosju kronor**
   Byxorna är billiga och kostar 327 kr.
   TRANSLATION: *The trousers are cheap and cost 327 kr.*

5. **1 295 kr: tolvhundranittiofem kronor / etttusentvåhun-**
   dranittiofem kronor
   895 kr: åttahundranittiofem kronor
   Halsbandet brukade kosta 1 295 kr men på rea kostar det
   bara 895 kr.
   TRANSLATION: *The necklace used to cost 1295 kr, but on sale it only costs 895 kr.*

6. **femhundraåttiosju kronor**
   Taxiresan kostade 587 kr utan dricks.
   TRANSLATION: *The taxi ride cost 587 kr, tip not included.*

7. **åttahundrafemtio kronor**
   Svenska kräftor kostar 850 kr per kilo.
   TRANSLATION: *Swedish crayfish cost 850 kr per kilo.*

8. **hundratjugo kronor**
   Dagens lunch kostar 120 kr.
   TRANSLATION: *The lunch of the day costs 120 kr.*

9. **hundrasjuttiofem kronor**
   Biljetterna kostade 175 kr styck.
   TRANSLATION: *The tickets cost 175 kr each.*

10. **trettiofem kronor**
    En kaffe med påtår kostar 35 kr.
    TRANSLATION: *A coffee with refill costs 35 kr.*

VÅFFLOR
Taste Bud Tantaliser

1. 25 March.
2. Swedish waffles are thinner and heart-shaped.
3. The butter, which you melt in a saucepan.
4. Jam and ice cream.
5. **Smaklig måltid.**

ÖVERSÄTTNINGSÖVNING 3
Translation Challenge

1. Jag tycker att du är vacker och har vackra bruna ögon.

EXPLANATION:

- The verb **tycker** expresses your personal opinion, which nobody can disagree with.
- We use the adjective **vacker** twice in the sentence, but as it describes a different noun each time we need different endings. When we speak about a person, the adjective has a regular ending. However, when we describe a plural noun – in this case, "two eyes" – the adjective has to end with an -a: **vackra**. The same goes for **bruna**, which also refers to the eyes.

2. Vad åt du till frukost imorse / den här morgonen?

EXPLANATION:

- Both of these options are correct, but **imorse** is a single word you can use – instead of the longer phrase **den**

här morgonen – that also means "this morning". Make sure not to confuse it with **imorgon**, which means "tomorrow".

- **Åt** is the past tense of **att äta** and is irregular. Note that the **ä** of the infinitive becomes an **å** in the past tense.

3. Det ligger / Det är / Det finns fyra äpplen i en skål på bordet.

EXPLANATION:

- In this sentence, we can use the verbs **ligger** ("lie"), **är** ("are") or **finns** ("exist") interchangeably.
- The preposition **i** means "in" and **på** means "on": **i en skål** ("in a bowl") and **på bordet** ("on the table").
- Note that the plural ending for **ett äpple** is the slightly confusing **-en**.

4. Mina två danska vänner bor i Malmö.

EXPLANATION:

- The adjective **danska** needs to have an **-a** on the end, as it is referring to the plural "friends".
- Similarly, the word for "my" here is **mina**, as it also needs to have an **-a** on the end.

5. Har du ätit kräftor någon gång? / Har du någon gång ätit kräftor? / Har du någonsin ätit kräftor? / Har du ätit kräftor någonsin?

EXPLANATION:

- Just like in English, we use the perfect tense to ask if somebody "has done" something, but the simple past to ask if somebody "did" something. In this context, we are therefore using the perfect tense, unlike, for example, **åt du kräftor igår?** ("did you eat crayfish yesterday?").

- To translate "ever" in this context, we can use the time adverb **någon gång** ("sometimes") or **någonsin** ("ever"). These adverbs can be positioned at the end of the question or between the subject and the second verb.

ABBA
Famous Swedish Speakers

1. ABBA is an acronym consisting of the first letters of the members' names – Agnetha, Björn, Benny and Anni-Frid.
2. When they won the Eurovision Song Contest in 1974.
3. Due to marital problems.
4. Their divorce record.
5. They have created a show in London with avatars.

ANAGRAM 3
Jumbled Letters

1. **(en) surströmming** - fermented Baltic herring
   Here are some of the common words that can be made out of these letters:
   - **min** - mine
   - **(ett) rum** - room
   - **(ett) rör** - pipe

- **(en) ugn** - oven
- **ung** - young
- **(en) gris** - pig
- **(en) gröt** - porridge
- **gömt** - hidden
- **(en) röst** - voice
- **(ett) smör** - butter
- **(en) stig** - path
- **strö** - to strew
- **surt** - sour
- **grönt** - green
- **immun** - immune
- **(en) ström** - current
- **(ett) russin** - raisin
- **sömnig** - sleepy
- **smutsig** - dirty

2. **(en) sjuksköterska** - nurse
   - **resa** - to travel
   - **arket** - the sheet
   - **(en) kruka** - plant pot
   - **köket** - the kitchen
   - **rökte** - smoked
   - **rösta** - to vote
   - **saker** - things
   - **sjöar** - lakes
   - **stark** - strong
   - **(en) kaktus** - cactus
   - **(en) kassör** - cashier

- **skjuta** - to push
- **(en) skjuts** - ride
- **(en) strejk** - strike
- **justera** - to adjust
- **sjukast** - the sickest
- **skörast** - the most fragile
- **stressa** - to stress
- **skjutsar** - giving someone a lift

VIKTIGA DATUM
Number Focus

1. The Crown Princess of Sweden's birthday is **14 July**.
2. Every spring, Walpurgis Night is celebrated on **30 April**.
3. The writer Astrid Lindgren was born on **14 November 1907** in Småland.
4. Waffles are eaten on **25 March** because it is Waffle Day.
5. King Gustav Vasa died on **29 September 1560** in Stockholm.
6. Lucia is always celebrated on **13 December**.
7. Swedish National Day is on **6 June**.
8. Nobel Day is **10 December** and is celebrated in both Stockholm and Oslo.
9. Cinnamon Bun Day is celebrated on **4 October** every year.
10. Sweden has won the Eurovision Song Contest seven times: **1974, 1984, 1991, 1999, 2012, 2015** and **2023**.

KÄRLEKSMUMS
Taste Bud Tantaliser

1. Jag **sätter** ugnen på 175°C.
2. Jag **lägger** bakplåtspapper i en form.
3. Jag **smälter** smöret, **häller** i mjölken och **låter** det svalna.
4. Jag **vispar** ägg och socker riktigt pösigt med elvisp.
5. Jag **blandar** vetemjöl, vaniljsocker, kakao, bakpulver och salt.
6. Jag **tillsätter** smör och mjölk och **blandar** allt till en jämn smet. Jag **häller** smeten i formen.
7. Jag **gräddar** kakan i mitten av ugnen i 25 minuter. Jag **låter** kakan svalna.
8. Jag **smälter** smöret i en kastrull och **tar** det från värmen. Jag **tillsätter** övriga ingredienser och **rör** till en jämn smet.
9. Jag **brer** glasyren över den avsvalnade kakan och **strör** över kokosflingorna.
10. Jag **ställer** kakan kallt tills glasyren stelnat. Jag **skär** kärleksmumsen i bitar.

ÖVERSÄTTNINGSÖVNING 4
Translation Challenge

1. Hur stavas hans efternamn? / Hur stavar man hans efternamn?

EXPLANATION:

- Both of these constructions are correct.
- To create the passive form of the verb (to literally mean "is spelled"), we need to add an -s to the infinitive.
- Alternatively, you can use **man**, a general "you". **Man** is the subject (like saying "how does one spell his surname?") and we therefore use the regular present tense verb **stavar**.

2. Karlstad ligger i västra Sverige.

EXPLANATION:

- When describing where something is situated geographically, the verb **ligger** is always used, rather than **är**.
- **Västra** is an adjective and, as it is modifying a definite noun (the western part of Sweden), it needs an -a on the end.

3. Fåglarna sjunger så vackert på våren.

EXPLANATION:

- Adverbs that describe how something is done often end in "-ly" in English: for example "quickly", "carefully", "beautifully". To form this type of adverb in Swedish, start with the adjective and add -t. For example, **försiktig** ("careful") becomes **försiktigt** ("carefully"), and **vacker** ("beautiful") becomes **vackert** ("beautifully").
- Pay attention to the preposition and the ending of the noun in the phrase **på våren** ("in the spring"). To talk generally about a limited time period (here, "any / every

spring", rather than "this spring"), we always use **på** and the definite form: **på vintern** ("in the winter"), **på påsken** ("at Easter"), **på julen** ("at Christmas").

4. Har du förlovat dig / ni förlovat er? Grattis!

EXPLANATION:

- **Att förlova sig** is a verb that always needs a reflexive pronoun. If we're asking the question to one person (**du**), we'll use the reflexive pronoun **dig**. If we're asking a couple, (the plural "you", **ni**), we'll use the reflexive pronoun **er**.
- **Grattis** is spelled with a double -**tt**-, which means the -**a**- is pronounced as a short vowel. **Gratis**, with one -**t**-, means "free", and the -**a**- is pronounced as a long vowel.

5. I somras åkte jag till Sverige på semester. / Jag åkte på semester till Sverige i somras.

EXPLANATION:

- Both of these options are correct. Just pay attention to the sentence structure if you started the sentence with **i somras** ("this summer"), as the order of the verb and subject is reversed.
- Compare **i somras** with **på våren** ("in the spring"), which we saw in sentence 3 of this activity. To refer to a specific time in the past that happened this year (for example "this summer", rather than just any summer), we use the preposition **i** and add an -**s**: for example **i julas** ("this Christmas"), **i påskas** ("this Easter"), **i vintras** ("this winter").

ALFRED NOBEL
Famous Swedish Speakers

1. Swedish, Russian, English, French, German and Italian.
2. People who improved the world through literature, chemistry, medicine, physics and peace.
3. 1901.
4. Alfred Nobel died on that date.
5. On **Stortorget** (the main square) in the Old Town in Stockholm.

ANAGRAM 4
Jumbled Letters

1. **(en) kanelbulle** - cinnamon bun

   While there are many words that can be made out of these letters, here are some of the most common ones:
   - **(ett) ben** - leg, bone
   - **(en) eka** - rowing boat
   - **kul** - fun
   - **len** - soft
   - **(en) ull** - wool
   - **(en) bula** - bump
   - **eken** - the oak
   - **elak** - mean
   - **kall** - cold
   - **klen** - weak
   - **leka** - to play
   - **neka** - to refuse

- **(en) ankel** - ankle
- **blank** - shiny
- **(en) bunke** - bowl
- **enkla** - simple (plural)
- **(en) kabel** - cable
- **(en) nalle** - teddy bear
- **blekna** - to fade
- **kullen** - the hill

2. **(en) lingonsylt** - lingonberry jam
- **log** (from **att le**) - smiled
- **(en) nos** - animal nose, snout
- **(ett) ont** - pain
- **(en) ost** - cheese
- **(en) sol** - sun
- **(en) ton** - tone
- **(en) lins** - lens
- **(en) logi** - accommodation
- **noll** - nil
- **(en) sill** - herring
- **(en) stil** - style
- **(en) stol** - chair
- **(en) insyn** - insight
- **(ett) intyg** - permit
- **solig** - sunny
- **(ett) stygn** - stitch
- **tills** - until
- **yngst** - youngest
- **ytlig** - shallow
- **osynlig** - invisible

NÄR FYLLER ALVA ÅR?
Number Focus

EXERCISE 1 - FIND THE NUMBERS

1. 73
2. 11 June
3. 22 and 14
4. 4th
5. 1:30pm

JANSSONS FRESTELSE
Taste Bud Tantaliser

FILL IN THE PREPOSITIONS

1. Sätt ugnen **på** 200°C.
2. Skala och skär löken **i** tunna skivor.
3. Fräs den mjuk **i** lite smör **i** en stekpanna.
4. Skala potatisen och skär den **i** tunna strimlor.
5. Smörj en ugnssäker form.
6. Lägg **i** ett lager potatis, därefter lök, ansjovis och sedan resten av potatisen. Häll **på** grädde och mjölk. Strö över ströbrödet.
7. Grädda din Jansson **i** nedre delen av ugnen 45–50 minuter.
8. Smaklig måltid!

COMPREHENSION QUESTIONS

1. Christmas, Easter and as a dish on a smörgåsbord.
2. "Temptation".
3. Fry it in butter until soft.
4. Breadcrumbs.
5. The lower part of the oven.

15-MINUTE COFFEE BREAKS

CHECKLIST
15-MINUTE COFFEE BREAKS

Reading Focus
❏ Vasaloppet - page 170
❏ Midsommar - page 185
❏ Fredagsmys - page 201

Grammar Focus
❏ Vill du gifta dig med mig? - page 175
❏ Tycka, tro och tänka - page 191
❏ Adjektiv - page 205
❏ Tid och plats - page 215

Vocabulary Consolidation
❏ Att laga och äta mat - page 179
❏ Sport - page 196
❏ Arbete - page 210

41

VASALOPPET
READING FOCUS

In this activity we're focusing on a reading text about the cross-country skiing race **Vasaloppet**. As you read it, it's a good idea to note down any words and phrases that are new to you, to help you remember them. After you have read the text as many times as you need to, complete the exercises that follow to test your understanding. **Lycka till!**

* * *

Before we start, a quick note about the measurement of distances in Swedish. In Sweden, large distances are measured in **mil** – the equivalent to 10 kilometres. You'll notice this when the length of **Vasaloppet** is mentioned.

Svenskar älskar vintersport. I februari har alla skolor ett lov som heter "sportlov" då många svenska familjer åker till fjällen för att åka skidor. Både längd- och utförsåkning är populära aktiviteter och det är inte konstigt att Sverige har världens största och äldsta tävling i längdskidåkning. Tävlingen heter Vasaloppet efter kungen Gustav Vasa. När Gustav Vasa var en ung man på 1500-talet åkte han skidor samma sträcka som tävlingen eftersom han var jagad av danska soldater.

Tävlingen började 1922 och bara 119 personer deltog i loppet, men tävlingen har blivit mer populär för varje år. Vem som helst kan anmäla sig till Vasaloppet och många kända personer och idrottare har åkt det t. ex. har både den svenska kungen och prinsen åkt Vasaloppet.

Loppet går av stapeln varje år den första söndagen i mars och är en folkfest och nu för tiden är det 15 800 skidåkare som deltar. Loppet börjar i skidorten Sälen och slutar i staden Mora. Det är 9 mil mellan de båda orterna så det är ett långt och tungt lopp. Den snabbaste Vasaloppsåkaren i historien är den norska skidåkaren Tord Asle Gjerdalen. 2021 åkte han Vasaloppet på 3 timmar och 28 minuter men de flesta åker mycket långsammare.

Vasaloppet är en del av fyra svenska tävlingar som kallas "en svensk klassiker". På 12 månader ska man åka Vasaloppet, cykla Vätternrundan, simma Vansbrosimningen och springa Lidingöloppet. Det är väldigt jobbigt att göra en svensk klassiker men ca 10.000 amatörer gör den varje år och tävlingarna blir mer och mer populära.

VOCABULARY
(ett) lov - school break
(en) längdskidåkning - cross-country skiing
(en) utförsåkning - downhill skiing

största (stor, större, störst) - the largest
äldsta (gammal, äldre, äldst) - the oldest
(en) sträcka - distance
att delta - to participate
(en) tävling - competition
att anmäla - to register
(en) idrottare - athlete
t. ex. (till exempel) - for example
(en) skidåkare - skier
(en) skidort - ski resort
jobbigt - tough, hard
snabbaste (snabb, snabbare, snabbast) - the fastest
norsk - Norwegian
långsammare (långsamt, långsammare, långsammast) -
slower
ca (circa) - circa, approximately

EXERCISE 1 - COMPREHENSION

Answer the following questions in English.

1. Why did Gustav Vasa ski between Sälen and Mora?

    _____

   _____

2. When does **Vasaloppet** take place?

    _____

   _____

3. How long is **Vasaloppet**?

✎ _____

_____

4. Where is the fastest **Vasaloppet** skier from?

✎ _____

_____

5. What kind of sports are included in the Swedish Classic Circuit?

✎ _____

_____

EXERCISE 2 - FIND THE SWEDISH

In the text, find the Swedish translation of the following words and phrases. Note that they are not listed in the order in which they appear in the text.

1. the mountains

✎ _____

2. the world's largest

✎ _____

3. anybody

✎ _____

4. fastest

   ✎_____

5. slower

   ✎_____

6. a long and strenuous race

   ✎_____

7. famous people

   ✎_____

8. it is not surprising / strange

   ✎_____

9. takes place

   ✎_____

10. nowadays

   ✎_____

* * *

Bra jobbat! When you have completed the two exercises, you can turn to page 221 to check your answers.

42

VILL DU GIFTA DIG MED MIG?

GRAMMAR FOCUS

In this activity we will look at reflexive verbs. We'll start with a short explanation, then complete the exercises that follow to test your understanding.

* * *

Reflexive verbs are verbs that must be used with a reflexive pronoun. The pronoun changes depending on the subject of the verb. Let's take the example of the verb **att tvätta sig**, meaning "to wash oneself". Pay attention to the reflexive pronouns, which are in italics:

Jag tvättar *mig*.	I wash *myself*.
Du tvättar *dig*.	You wash *yourself*.
Han tvättar *sig*.	He washes *himself*.
Hon tvättar *sig*.	She washes *herself*.
Vi tvättar *oss*.	We wash *ourselves*.
Ni tvättar *er*.	You wash *yourselves*.
De tvättar *sig*.	They wash *themselves*.

Att tvätta sig is easy to translate as it is a reflexive verb in both Swedish and English. However, there are many Swedish reflexive verbs that are not reflexive in English. One example that you will have come across early in your Swedish learning is **att lära sig** ("to learn"), for example in **jag lär mig svenska** ("I'm learning Swedish"). While there is no reflexive idea in English ("myself"), the reflexive pronoun **mig** is essential in this phrase in Swedish. Watch out for other verbs like this throughout this activity.

Now let's look at some common reflexive verbs and practise using them. **Nu börjar vi!**

EXERCISE 1 - CHOOSE THE PRONOUN

Here are five reflexive verbs. Read the sentences and fill in each gap with the relevant reflexive pronoun.

1. **att ha på sig** - to wear
   Ska du ha på ✎_____ den gula klänningen på bröllopet?
2. **att gifta sig** - to get married
   Lars och Stina ska gifta ✎_____ i kyrkan.
3. **att lära sig** - to learn
   Jag vill lära ✎_____ både svenska och danska.
4. **att klippa sig** - to get a haircut
   Åke måste gå till frisören och klippa ✎_____ . Han är så långhårig!
5. **att höra av sig** - to get in touch
   Vad trevligt att ni hörde av ✎_____ !

EXERCISE 2 - FIND THE REFLEXIVE VERBS

Read the text and circle all the reflexive verbs you see.

Jag vaknar varje morgon och tvättar mig i ansiktet och borstar mina tänder. Efter det klär jag på mig och tar en promenad. Sedan sätter jag mig ner vid frukostbordet och tar mig en kopp kaffe. På kvällen, när jag är trött efter en lång dag, kopplar jag av genom att lägga mig ner i min säng och sova.

EXERCISE 3 - WRITING CHALLENGE

Below are five other common reflexive verbs. For each one, write a sentence that includes the verb and uses the simple past tense.

I. **att förlova sig** - to get engaged

✎ _____

_____

_____

2. **att kamma sig** - to comb one's hair

✎ _____

_____

_____

3. **att koncentrera sig** - to concentrate

✎_____

_____

_____

4. **att bestämma sig** - to decide

✎_____

_____

_____

5. **att skilja sig** - to get divorced

✎_____

_____

_____

* * *

Jättebra! We hope that you are now more confident using reflexive verbs and are happy with your answers. Turn to page 222 to see how you got on.

43

ATT LAGA OCH ÄTA MAT
VOCABULARY CONSOLIDATION

This activity will help you expand your vocabulary on the topic of food. Take your time to familiarise yourself with the words and phrases listed below. Then, cover up the list with your hand or a piece of paper and try to complete the exercises that follow without looking at it. **Lycka till!**

* * *

allergisk - allergic
att diska - to wash up
att duka - to set the table
(en) frukost - breakfast
(en) gaffel - fork
hälsosam - healthy
(en) kastrull - pot, saucepan
(en) kniv - knife
att koka - to boil
att laga mat - to cook

(en) matsäck - packed lunch
(ett) mellanmål - snack
(en) middag - dinner
mätt - full
ohälsosam - unhealthy
salt - salty
(en) sked - spoon
(en) skål - bowl
sur - sour
(en) tallrik - plate

EXERCISE 1 - TRANSLATE

Have a look at these English words from the vocabulary list and write down the Swedish translation. Try not to refer back to the list.

1. a fork

   ✎_____

2. to boil

   ✎_____

3. unhealthy

   ✎_____

4. a plate

   ✎_____

5. full

✎_____

EXERCISE 2 - WHAT AM I?

Give the Swedish word for what is being described in each sentence below.

1. Man äter den här maten mellan lunch och middag.

   ✎_____

2. Man använder den på spisen och man kan koka vatten i den.

   ✎_____

3. Man lägger tallrikar, glas, knivar och gafflar på ett bord innan man ska äta.

   ✎_____

4. Den är rund och man kan äta soppa eller efterrätt med den.

   ✎_____

5. Den är lång och vass och man kan skära mat med den.

   ✎_____

EXERCISE 3 - UNSCRAMBLE

Each group of words below will form a sentence on the topic of food. Put the words in the right order to form correct sentences.

1. mat om tycker Sofia laga inte att

   ✎ _____

   _____

2. ta matsäck på barnen sig med onsdag måste

   ✎ _____

   _____

3. är allergisk mot både nötter och mjölkprodukter Erik

   ✎ _____

   _____

4. popcorn de skål med TV:n salta åt framför en

   ✎ _____

   _____

5. sura att smakade Albin det äpplet tyckte gott

   ✎ _____

   _____

EXERCISE 4 - BACK IN TIME

Rewrite the following sentences in the simple past tense.

1. Anders äter frukost på hotellet innan han checkar ut.

   🖊_____

   _____

   _____

2. Linn lagar hälsosam mat till hela familjen.

   🖊_____

   _____

   _____

3. De är mätta och diskar tallrikarna efter middagen.

   🖊_____

   _____

   _____

4. Erik dukar bordet med glas, tallrikar och bestick.

   🖊_____

   _____

   _____

5. Mattias kokar potatisen i en kastrull.

_____

_____

_____

* * *

Jättebra! Once you are happy with your answers, you can check them on page 223.

44

MIDSOMMAR
READING FOCUS

In this Reading Focus activity we'll be finding out about how midsummer is celebrated in Sweden while practising our reading and translation skills. Read the text below, using the vocabulary list to help you, then complete the exercises that follow.

* * *

Traditionellt firas midsommarafton på årets längsta dag. Förutom julen är midsommar den viktigaste högtiden för svenskar på hela året. Midsommar symboliserar början på sommaren med lång semester, bad och solsken.

Fram till 1952 var midsommarafton alltid den 23 juni. Nu firas den alltid på en fredag och kan vara mellan den 20 och 26 juni.

På midsommarafton samlas många familjer och vänner för att fira tillsammans. Det äts traditionell sommarmat som sill, färskpotatis och jordgubbstårta till efterrätt. Ofta spelar man spel och leker under dagen. På förmiddagen klär man en stång med löv och blommor, det kallas en midsommarstång. Man gör kransar av blommor att ha i håret, midsommarkransar. Både midsommarstången och kransen symboliserar sommarens grönska. Ofta spelar folkmusiker under midsommarfirandet och man dansar runt midsommarstången. Den mest berömda dansen heter "Små grodorna", då hoppar alla runt och leker att de är grodor.

Det finns många myter om midsommarnatten. Till exempel, om man lägger sju olika blommor under huvudkudden så drömmer man om den person man kommer att gifta sig med.

Man firar midsommar i hela Sverige men många åker till Dalarna eller ut i skärgården. Städerna kan kännas tomma. Men om du är i Stockholm firas alltid riktig traditionell midsommar på Skansen.

VOCABULARY

(en) högtid - holiday, festival
(en) semester - holiday
(en) midsommarstång - maypole
(en) krans - wreath
att leka - to play
(en) grönska - greenery
små grodorna - the little frogs
(en) myt - myth
(en) huvudkudde - pillow

att drömma - dream
Dalarna - a Swedish county
(en) skärgården - archipelago
tom - empty

EXERCISE 1 - COMPREHENSION

Answer the following questions in English.

1. On which day was Midsummer's Eve traditionally celebrated?

   ✎_____

   _____

2. What date is Midsummer's Eve?

   ✎_____

   _____

3. What do people eat for dessert at midsummer?

   ✎_____

   _____

4. What does the midsummer maypole symbolise?

   ✎_____

   _____

5. Name two places where many Swedes celebrate midsummer.

✎_____

_____

EXERCISE 2 - SANT ELLER FALSKT?

Read the following statements about midsummer and decide whether they are **sant** ("true") or **falskt** ("false"). Circle your answer and, if it is false, correct the statement.

1. One of the traditions is to jump around and pretend to be animals.
   SANT | FALSKT

   ✎_____

   _____

2. People eat ham and cabbage at midsummer.
   SANT | FALSKT

   ✎_____

   _____

3. Midsummer's Eve is on the same day of the week every year.
   SANT | FALSKT

   ✎_____

   _____

4. If you sleep with flowers under your pillow, you will dream about the person you will marry.

SANT | FALSKT

✎ _____

_____

5. Many Swedes celebrate midsummer in Stockholm.

SANT | FALSKT

✎ _____

_____

EXERCISE 3 - TRANSLATE

Translate the following sentences about midsummer into Swedish, using vocabulary from the text.

1. Many families get together to celebrate.

✎ _____

_____

_____

2. You dance around the maypole.

✎ _____

_____

_____

3. Midsummer is the most important holiday in Sweden.

✎_____

_____

_____

4. You play games during the day.

✎_____

_____

_____

5. The most famous dance is called "the little frogs".

✎_____

_____

_____

* * *

When you're ready, you can check your answers on page 225.

45

TYCKA, TRO OCH TÄNKA

GRAMMAR FOCUS

In this Grammar Focus activity we'll be focusing on three particular verbs: **tycka, tro** and **tänka**. These verbs can be tricky for English speakers as they can all be translated as "to think", but they are used in different ways and are not interchangeable. Read the explanation below to learn about when to use each verb, then test your knowledge in the exercises that follow. **Då sätter vi igång!**

* * *

ATT TYCKA

Att tycka is used to express a personal opinion – something that people can't disagree with because an opinion is subjective. For example:

Märta tycker att sill smakar gott.
Märta thinks that pickled herring tastes good. (It is Märta's opinion that pickled herring tastes good.)

Sixten can't disagree with that because it's Märta's taste. However, Sixten can reply saying that he doesn't think pickled herring tastes good. Then, we could also say:

Sixten tycker inte att sill smakar gott.
Sixten doesn't think that pickled herring tastes good.
(In Sixten's opinion, pickled herring doesn't taste good.)

Here's another example of **tycker:**

Jag tycker boken var jättebra.
I think the book was great.

ATT TRO

Att tro, on the other hand, is used to express something that you are not sure about, or that is not supported by any evidence or experience. Let's see some examples:

Olle tror att sill smakar gott.
Olle thinks that pickled herring tastes good. (Olle thinks that pickled herring tastes good, but he hasn't tried it yet, so he can't be sure.)

Jag tror att det kommer att regna snart.
I think it will start to rain soon.

ATT TÄNKA

Att tänka is used to describe having a thought or thinking about something in the sense of having it on your mind. For example:

Linnea tänker på sill.
Linnea is thinking about pickled herring.

Jag tänker på min pojkvän.
I'm thinking about my boyfriend.

Att tänka is also used to express an intention – something that you are planning to do in the future:

Märta tänker äta sill när hon är i Sverige.
Märta is planning to eat pickled herring when she is in Sweden.

Jag tänker studera svenska.
I'm planning to study Swedish.

Now that we've seen some examples, put what you've learned into practice by completing the following exercises. **Lycka till!**

EXERCISE 1 - FILL IN THE GAPS

Fill in the gap in each sentence using the correct form of **tycka, tro** or **tänka**.

1. Jag ✎_____ att solskenet är härligt.
2. Vad ✎_____ du på?
3. ✎_____ du att det blir fint väder i helgen?
4. Vad ✎_____ du göra i sommar?
5. Vilken tröja ✎_____ du att jag passar bäst i?
6. Vi ✎_____ flytta till Göteborg nästa år.
7. Jag ✎_____ att hon är sjuk.
8. Jag ✎_____ att det blir regn i morgon.

9. Vi måste ✎_____ positivt!
10. Jag ✎_____ att de passar bra ihop.

EXERCISE 2 - TRANSLATE

Translate the following sentences into Swedish using the correct forms of **tycka, tro** or **tänka**.

1. Do you think Andreas likes Eva?

    ✎_____

    _____

    _____

2. She thinks that she will get the job.

    ✎_____

    _____

    _____

3. I think Malmö FF is the better team.

    ✎_____

    _____

    _____

4. They are planning to go to the cinema tomorrow.

_____

_____

_____

5. I think about you every day.

_____

_____

_____

* * *

When you're happy with your answers, turn to page 226 to check them.

46

SPORT
VOCABULARY CONSOLIDATION

For this Vocabulary Consolidation, we've chosen 20 words or phrases on the topic of sport. Take some time to familiarise yourself with the vocabulary list, then cover it up and try to complete the exercises without referring back to it. **Lycka till!**

* * *

att byta om - to get changed
(en) friidrott - athletics
(ett) gym - gym
inomhus - indoors
att klättra - to climb
(ett) landslag - national team
(ett) lopp - race
löparskor (en word) - running shoes
(ett) omklädningsrum - changing room
att paddla kajak - to kayak
(en) simbassäng - swimming pool

att simma - to swim

att spela ishockey - to play ice hockey

att stretcha - to stretch

att träna - to train, to practise, to exercise

(en) träning - training session

utomhus - outdoors

(en) utrustning - gear, equipment

att åka skidor - to ski

att åka skridskor - to ice skate

EXERCISE 1 - TRANSLATE

Write the Swedish translation of the following pieces of vocabulary. Try not to refer back to the list.

1. to swim

   ✎ _____

2. indoors

   ✎ _____

3. gear, equipment

   ✎ _____

4. to ski

   ✎ _____

5. to get changed

   ✎ _____

EXERCISE 2 - FILL IN THE GAPS

Fill in the gap in each sentence below using a word or phrase from the vocabulary list.

1. Barnen leker i vattnet, de älskar att vara i

   ✎_____ .

2. Jag åker till fjällen varje år för att

   ✎_____ .

3. Jag föredrar att spela ✎_____
   inomhus i ishallen eftersom det är så kallt

   ✎_____ mitt i vintern.

4. Man måste ha bra ✎_____ för att
   klättra i berg.

5. Zlatan Ibrahimović spelade i det svenska

   ✎_____ i fotboll.

EXERCISE 3 - TRANSLATE INTO ENGLISH

Translate these five sentences into English.

1. Niklas har paddlat kajak sedan han var liten.

   ✎_____

   _____

   _____

2. Jag behöver nya löparskor innan loppet på lördag.

   ✎_____

   _____

   _____

3. Hela laget var i omklädningsrummet innan träningen började.

   _____

   _____

   _____

4. Jag tycker om att åka skridskor på sjön.

   _____

   _____

   _____

5. Man måste stretcha innan matchen.

   _____

   _____

   _____

EXERCISE 4 - PUT INTO PRACTICE

Use the vocabulary from the list to help you translate these sentences into Swedish.

1. The gym opens at 8 o'clock on Saturdays.

   _____

   _____

   _____

2. I exercise four times a week. I run on Mondays and Thursdays, play football / soccer on Wednesdays and swim at the weekend.

✎ _____

_____

_____

3. I want to try climbing.

✎ _____

_____

_____

4. I like to watch athletics on TV.

✎ _____

_____

_____

5. Åsa swims every morning before she goes to work.

✎ _____

_____

_____

* * *

Strålande! When you're ready, you can check your answers to the exercises on page 227.

47

FREDAGSMYS
READING FOCUS

In this activity we will read and learn about the modern traditions of **fredagsmys** and **tacofredag**. Read the text as many times as you need to, then answer the comprehension questions and complete the vocabulary and preposition exercises. **Lycka till!**

* * *

Vad gör vanliga svenskar en fredagkväll? Ja, istället för att ta en öl med sina arbetskamrater eller träffa vänner på restaurang är det en stor chans att man är hemma och myser med sin familj. Svenskar vill ofta koppla av efter en stressig arbetsvecka. Det är så vanligt att vanan har fått ett namn, det heter fredagsmys. Sedan 2006 finns ordet till och med i ordboken.

Vanligtvis börjar fredagsmyset med att man köper eller lagar något gott att äta, som till exempel tacos eller pizza.

Ibland kallas fredagar även "tacofredag" i Sverige för att det är så populärt att äta tacos på fredagar. Sverige och Norge äter mest tacos i hela Europa.

Efter middagen myser man i soffan med familj eller vänner. Man dukar upp chips, dipp och läsk på vardagsrumsbordet. Man spelar ett spel eller så sätter man på en bra film eller TV-serie.

Fredagsmys är nu en viktig del av svensk kultur och kanske visar hur svenskar prioriterar familj och nära relationer. Det är ett sätt att avsluta en stressig vecka och göra sig redo för en trevlig helg.

VOCABULARY

vanlig - common
att mysa - to be cosy
att koppla av - to relax
(en) vana - habit
till och med - even
(en) ordbok - dictionary
vanligtvis - usually
att duka upp - to set the table, to lay out
(ett) vardagsrumsbord - coffee table
nära relationer (en word) - close relationships
att avsluta - to end

EXERCISE I - COMPREHENSION

Answer the following questions in English.

1. What do many Swedes do on a Friday night?

   ✎ _____

   _____

2. Why do they do this?

   ✎ _____

   _____

3. What is popular to eat for dinner on Fridays?

   ✎ _____

   _____

4. What activities might you do after dinner as part of **fredagsmys**?

   ✎ _____

   _____

5. What can **fredagsmys** teach us about Swedish culture?

   ✎ _____

   _____

EXERCISE 2 - VOCABULARY

Fill in the gap in each sentence below with an appropriate word or phrase from the vocabulary list.

1. Jag har som ✎_____ att simma en gång i veckan.
2. Jag behöver en svensk ✎_____ för att förbättra min svenska.
3. Håkan ✎_____ kaffe och kakor i fikarummet.
4. Ska vi äta middag vid ✎_____ så vi kan titta på TV?
5. Jag vill bara ✎_____ den här helgen!

EXERCISE 3 - PREPOSITIONS

Look at the following extracts from the text. Fill in the missing preposition **i** ("in") or **på** ("on").

1. träffa vänner ✎_____ en restaurang
2. finns ordet till och med ✎_____ ordboken
3. att äta tacos ✎_____ fredagar
4. Sverige och Norge äter mest tacos ✎_____ hela Europa
5. efter middagen myser man ✎_____ soffan

* * *

Bra jobbat! When you're finished, turn to the answers section on page 229.

48

ADJEKTIV
GRAMMAR FOCUS

In this Grammar Focus we're looking at adjectives and how they change depending on the noun they describe. Read the explanation below, then put your learning into practice in the exercises that follow.

* * *

Articles play an important part in Swedish grammar. In Swedish, adjectives change depending on whether the noun they refer to is an **en** noun, an **ett** noun or is plural. Take a look at these examples:

en stor bil
a big car

ett stort hus
a big house

två stora hundar
two big dogs

Adjectives also change if the noun is used in its definite form. In this case, we add -**a** to the end of the adjective and add **den**, **det** or **de** in front of the adjective. For example:

den stora bilen
the big car

det stora huset
the big house

de stora hundarna
the big dogs

Finally, let's see what happens when adjectives are used with nouns in a possessive form. In this case, we start with the word for "my", "your", etc. and then add the adjective in the form ending in -**a**. For example:

min stora bil
my big car

ditt stora hus
your big house

våra stora hundar
our big dogs

There are some irregular adjectives (e.g. **liten, litet, små** – small). However, the good news is that most adjectives follow the same pattern, so the more you practise applying these rules to adjectives, the more natural it will become. **Så nu övar vi!**

EXERCISE 1 - FIND THE ADJECTIVES

Read the text and circle all the adjectives you see.

Igår gick jag på bio och såg en fantastisk men sorglig film med mina vänner. Det var en enorm, modern biograf med en stor duk som visade den romantiska filmen i hög kvalitet. Salongen var stor och bekväm med mjuka, röda stolar. Ljudet var klart och högt och musiken var dramatisk och intensiv. Filmen var full av dramatiska scener, vackra landskap och intressanta karaktärer.

EXERCISE 2 - FILL IN THE GAPS

Complete each sentence with the adjective(s) given in brackets. Watch out for your adjective endings.

1. Jag är nöjd med min ✎_____ bil. [**billig** - cheap]

2. ✎_____ kaffe får mig att vakna till liv. [**stark** - strong]

3. En ✎_____ kattunge lekte med en ✎_____ boll. [**söt** - cute], [**mjuk** - soft]

4. ✎_____ luft gör mig ✎_____ [**frisk** - fresh], [**pigg** - alert]

5. Ett ✎_____ ✎_____ glas
vatten var precis vad jag behövde! [**stor** - large],
[**kall** - cold]

EXERCISE 3 - REWRITE THE SENTENCES

Rewrite the following sentences, changing the nouns into their definite forms.

1. Vill du ha rött eller vitt vin?

   ✎_____

   _____

2. De bor i ett gult hus.

   ✎_____

   _____

3. Hon fick en stor fin blomma när hon fyllde år.

   ✎_____

   _____

4. Emma har en grön och röd klänning på sig.

   ✎_____

   _____

5. Köper du nya skor?

✎ _____

_____

EXERCISE 4 - TRANSLATE

Translate the following phrases into Swedish.

1. their cute dog

✎ _____

2. my brown hair

✎ _____

3. her beautiful voice

✎ _____

4. your new TV [singular "your"]

✎ _____

5. our nice house

✎ _____

* * *

Utmärkt! You can check your answers on page 230.

49

ARBETE

VOCABULARY CONSOLIDATION

In this Vocabulary Consolidation activity we are learning and practising vocabulary relating to work. Read through the vocabulary list as many times as you need to in order to familiarise yourself with any words that are new to you. When you are ready, cover up the list and complete the exercises that follow. **Redo? Låt oss börja!**

* * *

(en) arbetskamrat - colleague, co-worker

arbetslös - unemployed

(en) arbetsplats - place of work

(en) bibliotekarie - librarian

(en) chef - manager

(ett) fikarum - break room

(en) frisör - hairdresser

(en) författare - author

(en) förskollärare - nursery teacher

(en) föräldraledighet - parental leave
halvtid - part-time
(en) ingenjör - engineer
(en) jurist - solicitor
(en) läkare - doctor
(en) lärare - teacher
(en) personal - staff
(en) revisor - accountant
(en) taxichaufför - taxi driver
(en) trädgårdsmästare - gardener
(en) veterinär - vet

EXERCISE 1 - SANT ELLER FALSKT?

Read the descriptions and decide if the answer given is **sant** ("true") or **falskt** ("false"). Circle your answer.

1. This person works with law - **en ingenjör.**
   SANT | FALSKT
2. This person takes care of young children - **en förskollärare.**
   SANT | FALSKT
3. This person works in a kitchen - **en frisör.**
   SANT | FALSKT
4. This person works indoors - **en trädgårdsmästare.**
   SANT | FALSKT
5. This person writes books - **en författare.**
   SANT | FALSKT

EXERCISE 2 - MATCH

Which professions work with these plural nouns? Draw a line to match each profession with a noun.

bibliotekarie	saxar
frisör	elever
lärare	bilar
veterinär	böcker
taxichaufför	djur

EXERCISE 3 - FILL IN THE GAPS

Complete the sentences below by filling in each gap with one word from the vocabulary list.

1. Olle trivs på sin ✎_____ .

   TRANSLATION: *Olle likes his workplace.*

2. Robert och Karolina delar på

   ✎_____ .

   TRANSLATION: *Robert and Karolina share the parental leave.*

3. Lina har varit ✎_____

   i en månad.

   TRANSLATION: *Lina has been unemployed for a month.*

4. Anna utbildar sig till ✎_____ .

   TRANSLATION: *Anna is training to become an accountant.*

5. Jag är ✎_____ och ansvarig
för mycket ✎_____ .
TRANSLATION: *I am a manager and responsible for a lot of staff.*

EXERCISE 4 - UNSCRAMBLE

Put the words into the right order to make correct sentences.

1. arbeta jag halvtid vill

✎_____

_____

_____

2. skola som på Elin arbetar en lärare

✎_____

_____

_____

3. sin fantastiska Hannes arbetsplats har på
arbetskamrater

✎_____

_____

_____

4. i träffar Eva annan fikarummet jurist en

_____

_____

_____

5. drömmer Anders att läkare om bli

_____

_____

_____

* * *

Strålande! Now turn to page 232 to check your answers.

50

TID OCH PLATS
GRAMMAR FOCUS

In this activity we'll be practising a particular rule in Swedish grammar involving sentence structure. First, we'll review the rule, then we'll practise with some exercises.

* * *

In Swedish, when you start a sentence with a time phrase or a place, the sentence structure changes. The rule isn't complicated and you may already be familiar with it, as this reversed sentence structure is very common. The tricky part is remembering to do it.

Let's start with a regular sentence structure where the time or place is positioned at the end of the sentence:

Jag äter lunch med Nisse klockan halv tolv.
I eat lunch with Nisse at 11:30.

If we change the sentence so that it begins with the time phrase (**klockan halv tolv**), the subject, **jag**, and verb, **äter**, swap places. The correct sentence then looks like this:

Klockan halv tolv äter jag lunch med Nisse.
At 11:30 I eat lunch with Nisse.

EXERCISE 1 - TIME EXPRESSIONS

There are many ways of describing time. Translate the following sentences into English and see if you recognise the time expression at the start of each one.

1. Nuförtiden förstår jag mycket svenska.

    _____

    _____

    _____

2. Ibland pratar jag svenska med mina vänner.

    _____

    _____

    _____

3. Imorse åkte jag buss till jobbet.

    _____

    _____

    _____

4. Snart ska jag gå och lägga mig.

✎ _____

_____

_____

5. Varje tisdag äter jag middag med min mamma.

✎ _____

_____

_____

EXERCISE 2 - UNSCRAMBLE

Put the words into the right order to make a correct sentence. You can either start with the time / place or put the time / place at the end. Just make sure to adjust your sentence structure accordingly.

1. bodde i Kalmar först jag sju månader

✎ _____

_____

_____

2. jag på gatan en katt imorse såg

✎ _____

_____

_____

3. hela dagen de hemma i lördags var

  ✎ _____

_____

_____

4. åt under filmen popcorn vi

  ✎ _____

_____

_____

5. föräldrar besöka i helgen ska jag mina

  ✎ _____

_____

_____

EXERCISE 3 - REARRANGE

Change the sentence structure of each sentence by moving the time / place expression to the start.

1. Jag ska åka till Grekland imorgon.

  ✎ _____

_____

2. Vi talar svenska och engelska hemma.

✎ _____

_____

3. Apoteket öppnar klockan halv tio.

✎ _____

_____

4. Jag åt en kanelbulle till frukost imorse.

✎ _____

_____

5. Jag bor här.

✎ _____

_____

EXERCISE 4 - TRANSLATE

Finally, let's practise with some translations into Swedish. Write two versions of each sentence: one with the time / place phrase at the beginning and one with it at the end.

1. Sometimes I watch Swedish TV.

✎ _____

_____

_____

2. I eat lunch with my dad every Thursday.

   ✎_____

   _____

   _____

3. I'm going home soon.

   ✎_____

   _____

   _____

* * *

Nu var du duktig! When you've completed all the exercises, turn to page 233 to check your answers.

ANSWERS
15-MINUTE COFFEE BREAKS

VASALOPPET
Reading Focus

EXERCISE 1 - COMPREHENSION

1. He was chased by Danish soldiers.
2. On the first Sunday in March every year.
3. 90 kilometres / 9 Swedish **mil**.
4. Norway.
5. Skiing, cycling, swimming and running.

EXERCISE 2 - FIND THE SWEDISH

1. fjällen
2. världens största
3. vem som helst
4. snabbaste
5. långsammare
6. ett långt och tungt lopp
7. kända personer
8. det är inte konstigt
9. går av stapeln
10. nu för tiden

VILL DU GIFTA DIG MED MIG?
Grammar Focus

EXERCISE 1 - CHOOSE THE PRONOUN

1. Ska du ha på **dig** den gula klänningen på bröllopet?

   TRANSLATION: *Will you wear the yellow dress to the wedding?*

2. Lars och Stina ska gifta **sig** i kyrkan.

   TRANSLATION: *Lars and Stina are getting married in church.*

3. Jag vill lära **mig** både svenska och danska.

   TRANSLATION: *I want to learn both Swedish and Danish.*

4. Åke måste gå till frisören och klippa **sig**. Han är så långhårig!

   TRANSLATION: *Åke has to go to the hairdresser and get a haircut. He has such long hair!*

5. Vad trevligt att ni hörde av **er**!

   TRANSLATION: *How nice that you got in touch!*

EXERCISE 2 - FIND THE REFLEXIVE VERBS

Jag vaknar varje morgon och **tvättar mig** ("wash") i ansiktet och borstar mina tänder. Efter det **klär jag på mig** ("get dressed") och tar en promenad. Sedan **sätter jag mig ner** ("sit down") vid frukostbordet och **tar mig** ("have"*) en kopp kaffe. På kvällen, när jag är trött efter en lång dag, kopplar jag av genom att **lägga mig** ("lie down") ner i min säng och sova.

* In Swedish, **tar mig** is an idiomatic phrase meaning "have", as in "have a drink" or "have a snack", for example.

EXERCISE 3 - WRITING CHALLENGE

Here are some example sentences:

1. Vi förlovade oss igår.
   TRANSLATION: *We got engaged yesterday.*
2. Jag kammade mig imorse.
   TRANSLATION: *I combed my hair this morning.*
3. Åsa koncentrerade sig på provet.
   TRANSLATION: *Åsa concentrated on the test.*
4. Gustav bestämde sig för att åka på semester.
   TRANSLATION: *Gustav decided to go on holiday.*
5. Hennes föräldrar skilde sig förra året.
   TRANSLATION: *Her parents got divorced last year.*

ATT LAGA OCH ÄTA MAT
Vocabulary Consolidation

EXERCISE 1 - TRANSLATE

1. en gaffel
2. att koka
3. ohälsosam
4. en tallrik
5. mätt

EXERCISE 2 - WHAT AM I?

1. ett mellanmål
2. en kastrull
3. att duka

4. en sked
5. en kniv

EXERCISE 3 - UNSCRAMBLE

1. Sofia tycker inte om att laga mat.
   TRANSLATION: *Sofia doesn't like to cook.*
2. Barnen måste ta med sig matsäck på onsdag.
   TRANSLATION: *The children must bring a packed lunch on Wednesday.*
3. Erik är allergisk mot både nötter och mjölkprodukter.
   TRANSLATION: *Erik is allergic to both nuts and dairy.*
4. De åt en skål med salta popcorn framför TV:n.
   TRANSLATION: *They ate a bowl of salty popcorn in front of the TV.*
5. Albin tyckte att det sura äpplet smakade gott.
   TRANSLATION: *Albin thought the sour apple was tasty.*

EXERCISE 4 - BACK IN TIME

1. Anders åt frukost på hotellet innan han checkade ut.
   TRANSLATION: *Anders ate breakfast at the hotel before he checked out.*
2. Linn lagade hälsosam mat till hela familjen.
   TRANSLATION: *Linn cooked healthy food for the whole family.*
3. De var mätta och diskade tallrikarna efter middagen.
   TRANSLATION: *They were full and washed up the plates after dinner.*
4. Erik dukade bordet med glas, tallrikar och bestick.
   TRANSLATION: *Erik set the table with glasses, plates and cutlery.*

5. Mattias kokade potatisen i en kastrull.

TRANSLATION: *Mattias boiled the potatoes in a saucepan.*

MIDSOMMAR
Reading Focus

EXERCISE 1 - COMPREHENSION

1. On 23 June, which was considered the longest day of the year.
2. Nowadays, it's not on a fixed date. It's on a Friday between 20 and 26 June.
3. Strawberry cake.
4. The greenery of the summer.
5. The county of Dalarna or the archipelago.

EXERCISE 2 - SANT ELLER FALSKT?

1. Sant
2. Falskt – People eat pickled herring, new potatoes and strawberry cake at midsummer.
3. Sant
4. Sant (or at least according to the myth)
5. Falskt – Many Swedes celebrate midsummer in the county of Dalarna or in the archipelago.

EXERCISE 3 - TRANSLATE

1. Många familjer samlas för att fira.
2. Man dansar runt midsommarstången.
3. Midsommar är den viktigaste högtiden i Sverige.
4. Man spelar spel under dagen.
5. Den mest berömda dansen heter "små grodorna".

TYCKA, TRO OCH TÄNKA
Grammar Focus

EXERCISE 1 - FILL IN THE GAPS

1. Jag **tycker** att solskenet är härligt.
   TRANSLATION: *I think the sunshine is lovely.*

2. Vad **tänker** du på?
   TRANSLATION: *What are you thinking about?*

3. **Tror** du att det blir fint väder i helgen?
   TRANSLATION: *Do you think it will be nice weather this weekend?*

4. Vad **tänker** du göra i sommar?
   TRANSLATION: *What are your plans for the summer?*

5. Vilken tröja **tycker** du att jag passar bäst i?
   TRANSLATION: *Which jumper / sweater do you think suits me best?*

6. Vi **tänker** flytta till Göteborg nästa år.
   TRANSLATION: *We are planning to move to Gothenburg next year.*

7. Jag **tror** att hon är sjuk.
   TRANSLATION: *I think she is sick.*

8. Jag **tror** att det blir regn i morgon.
   TRANSLATION: *I think it will be rainy tomorrow.*

9. Vi måste **tänka** positivt!
   TRANSLATION: *We must think positively!*

10. Jag **tycker** att de passar bra ihop.
    TRANSLATION: *I think they suit each other.*

EXERCISE 2 - TRANSLATE

1. Tror du att Andreas tycker om Eva?
2. Hon tror att hon kommer att få jobbet.
3. Jag tycker att Malmö FF är det bättre laget.
4. De tänker gå på bio imorgon.
5. Jag tänker på dig varje dag.

SPORT
Vocabulary Consolidation

EXERCISE 1 - TRANSLATE

1. att simma
2. inomhus
3. utrustning
4. att åka skidor
5. att byta om

EXERCISE 2 - FILL IN THE GAPS

1. Barnen leker i vattnet, de älskar att vara i **simbassängen**.
   TRANSLATION: *The children are playing in the water. They love being in the swimming pool.*
2. Jag åker till fjällen varje år för att **åka skidor**.
   TRANSLATION: *I go to the mountains every year to ski.*
3. Jag föredrar att spela **ishockey** inomhus i ishallen eftersom det är så kallt **utomhus** mitt i vintern.
   TRANSLATION: *I prefer to play ice hockey indoors in the ice rink because it's so cold outdoors in the middle of winter.*

4. Man måste ha bra **utrustning** för att klättra i berg.
   TRANSLATION: *You must have good equipment to climb mountains.*

5. Zlatan Ibrahimović spelade i det svenska **landslaget** i fotboll.
   TRANSLATION: *Zlatan Ibrahimović played in the Swedish national football team.*

EXERCISE 3 - TRANSLATE INTO ENGLISH

1. Niklas has kayaked since he was little.
2. I need new running shoes before the race on Saturday.
3. The whole team was in the changing room before the training session began.
4. I like to (ice) skate on the lake.
5. You have to stretch before the match / game.

EXERCISE 4 - PUT INTO PRACTICE

1. Gymmet öppnar klockan åtta på lördagar.
2. Jag tränar fyra dagar i veckan. Jag springer på måndagar och torsdagar, spelar fotboll på onsdagar och simmar på helgen.
3. Jag vill prova / testa att klättra.
4. Jag gillar att titta / Jag tycker om att titta på friidrott på TV.
5. Åsa simmar varje morgon innan hon går till jobbet.

FREDAGSMYS
Reading Focus

EXERCISE 1 - COMPREHENSION

1. Go home and cosy up with their families.
2. They want to relax after a hard, working week.
3. Tacos.
4. Play games, or watch a film or TV series.
5. That it is family oriented and prioritises family and close friendships.

EXERCISE 2 - VOCABULARY

1. Jag har som **vana** att simma en gång i veckan.
   TRANSLATION: *I have a habit of going swimming once a week.*
2. Jag behöver en svensk **ordbok** för att förbättra min svenska.
   TRANSLATION: *I need a Swedish dictionary to improve my Swedish.*
3. Håkan **dukar upp** kaffe och kakor i fikarummet.
   TRANSLATION: *Håkan sets out coffee and biscuits in the break room.*
4. Ska vi äta middag vid **vardagsrumsbordet** så vi kan titta på TV?
   TRANSLATION: *Shall we have dinner at the coffee table so we can watch TV?*
5. Jag vill bara **koppla av** den här helgen!
   TRANSLATION: *I just want to relax this weekend!*

EXERCISE 3 - PREPOSITIONS

1. träffa vänner **på** en restaurang
   TRANSLATION: *meet friends at a restaurant*
2. finns ordet till och med **i** ordboken
   TRANSLATION: *the word is even in the dictionary*
3. att äta tacos **på** fredagar
   TRANSLATION: *to eat tacos on Fridays*
4. Sverige och Norge äter mest tacos **i** hela Europa
   TRANSLATION: *Sweden and Norway eat the most tacos in the whole of Europe*
5. efter middagen myser man **i** soffan
   TRANSLATION: *after dinner you cosy up on the sofa*

ADJEKTIV
Grammar Focus

EXERCISE 1 - FIND THE ADJECTIVES

Igår gick jag på bio och såg en **fantastisk** men **sorglig** film med mina vänner. Det var en **enorm**, **modern** biograf med en **stor** duk som visade den **romantiska** filmen i **hög** kvalitet. Salongen var **stor** och **bekväm** med **mjuka**, **röda** stolar. Ljudet var **klart** och **högt** och musiken var **dramatisk** och **intensiv**. Filmen var **full** av **dramatiska** scener, **vackra** landskap och **intressanta** karaktärer.

EXERCISE 2 - FILL IN THE GAPS

1. Jag är nöjd med min **billiga** bil.
   TRANSLATION: *I'm pleased with my cheap car.*

2. **Starkt** kaffe får mig att vakna till liv.

   TRANSLATION: *Strong coffee wakes me up.*

3. En **söt** kattunge lekte med en **mjuk** boll.

   TRANSLATION: *A cute kitten played with a soft ball.*

4. **Frisk** luft gör mig **pigg**.

   TRANSLATION: *Fresh air makes me alert.*

5. Ett **stort, kallt** glas vatten var precis vad jag behövde!

   TRANSLATION: *A large, cold glass of water was just what I needed!*

EXERCISE 3 - REWRITE THE SENTENCES

1. Vill du ha **det röda** eller **vita vinet?**

   TRANSLATION: *Would you like the red or the white wine?*

2. De bor i **det gula huset.**

   TRANSLATION: *They live in the yellow house.*

3. Hon fick **den stora fina blomman** när hon fyllde år.

   TRANSLATION: *She received the nice, big flower for her birthday.*

4. Emma har **den gröna** och **röda klänningen** på sig.

   TRANSLATION: *Emma is wearing the green and red dress.*

5. Köper du **de nya skorna?**

   TRANSLATION: *Are you buying the new shoes?*

EXERCISE 4 - TRANSLATE

1. deras söta / gulliga hund

2. mitt bruna hår

3. hennes vackra röst

4. din nya TV

5. vårt fina hus

ARBETE
Vocabulary Consolidation

EXERCISE 1 - SANT ELLER FALSKT?

1. Falskt
2. Sant
3. Falskt
4. Falskt
5. Sant

EXERCISE 2 - MATCH

bibliotekarie - böcker

frisör - saxar

lärare - elever

veterinär - djur

taxichaufför - bilar

EXERCISE 3 - FILL IN THE GAPS

1. Olle trivs på sin **arbetsplats**.
2. Robert och Karolina delar på **föräldraledigheten**.
3. Lina har varit **arbetslös** i en månad.
4. Anna utbildar sig till **revisor**.
5. Jag är **chef** och ansvarig för mycket **personal**.

EXERCISE 4 - UNSCRAMBLE

1. Jag vill arbeta halvtid.

   TRANSLATION: *I want to work part-time.*
2. Elin arbetar som lärare på en skola.

   TRANSLATION: *Elin works as a teacher in a school.*

3. Hannes har fantastiska arbetskamrater på sin arbetsplats.

   TRANSLATION: *Hannes has fantastic colleagues at his workplace.*

4. Eva träffar en annan jurist i fikarummet.

   TRANSLATION: *Eva meets another solicitor in the break room.*

5. Anders drömmer om att bli läkare.

   TRANSLATION: *Anders dreams of becoming a doctor.*

TID OCH PLATS
Grammar Focus

EXERCISE 1 - TIME EXPRESSIONS

1. Nowadays I understand a lot of Swedish.
2. Sometimes I speak Swedish with my friends.
3. This morning I took the bus to work.
4. Soon I will go to bed.
5. Every Tuesday I eat dinner with my mum.

EXERCISE 2 - UNSCRAMBLE

1. Först bodde jag sju månader i Kalmar. / Jag bodde först sju månader i Kalmar. / I Kalmar bodde jag först sju månader.

   TRANSLATION: *First I lived in Kalmar for seven months.*

2. Imorse såg jag en katt på gatan. / Jag såg en katt imorse på gatan. / På gatan imorse såg jag en katt.

   TRANSLATION: *This morning I saw a cat on the street.*

3. I lördags var de hemma hela dagen. / De var hemma hela dagen i lördags.

   TRANSLATION: *On Saturday, they were at home all day.*

4. Under filmen åt vi popcorn. / Vi åt popcorn under filmen.

   TRANSLATION: *During the film / movie, we ate popcorn.*

5. I helgen ska jag besöka mina föräldrar. / Jag ska besöka mina föräldrar i helgen.

   TRANSLATION: *This weekend I will visit my parents.*

EXERCISE 3 - REARRANGE

1. Imorgon ska jag åka till Grekland.

   TRANSLATION: *Tomorrow I'm going to Greece.*

2. Hemma talar vi svenska och engelska.

   TRANSLATION: *At home, we speak Swedish and English.*

3. Klockan halv tio öppnar apoteket.

   TRANSLATION: *At 9:30, the pharmacy opens.*

4. Imorse åt jag en kanelbulle till frukost.

   TRANSLATION: *This morning, I ate a cinnamon bun for breakfast.*

5. Här bor jag.

   TRANSLATION: *I live here.*

EXERCISE 4 - TRANSLATE

1. Ibland tittar jag på svensk TV. / Jag tittar på svensk TV ibland.

2. Jag äter lunch med min pappa varje torsdag. / Varje torsdag äter jag lunch med min pappa.

3. Jag går hem snart. / Snart går jag hem.

ACKNOWLEDGEMENTS

This book has very much been a team effort and I would like to take the opportunity to thank the people who have helped to put it together.

Firstly, thanks to Sarah Cole, Chloe West, Emma Green and the whole team at Teach Yourself. It's been a pleasure to work with you all and we'd like to thank you for your belief in the project and your enthusiasm for helping us bring Coffee Break to a new audience around the world.

Stort tack till Hanna Jedh who has brought her huge experience in teaching Swedish to learners around the world to the development of the activities in this book, helping you to practise and improve your Swedish in a fun and effective way.

We'd also like to thank Maurizio Verducci for his research and advice in the early stages of the project, and his role in the continued expansion of the *50 Coffee Breaks* series.

Tusen tack till Ava Dinwoodie, our Series Editor, whose dedication to the project and expert coordination meant that everyone knew exactly what they were doing and when it needed to be done!

Finally, thank you for reading the book and we very much hope that you have enjoyed building your skills in Swedish with us.

You may recall my mention of jazz virtuoso Charlie Parker in the Introduction to this book who, by focusing on practice, practice, practice, was then ready to fly and enjoy his performance. I hope that you're now feeling ready to let go and incorporate the new vocabulary, expressions and grammatical structures into your Swedish on a daily basis.

Mark Pentleton - Founder, Coffee Break Languages

SHARE YOUR THOUGHTS

If you'd like to help other learners like yourself discover Coffee Break Swedish, we'd be very grateful if you would consider leaving an honest review. If you bought the book online, you can do this easily by going to the website where you found it.

Tack! Thank you for sharing your thoughts and for helping other learners practise their Swedish on their Coffee Break.

MORE COFFEE BREAK LEARNING

Here at Coffee Break Languages we provide learning through podcasts, courses, videos and books. For more learning from Coffee Break Swedish visit coffeebreaklanguages.com/swedish.

Find us on Facebook, Twitter, Instagram, YouTube and TikTok for regular language-learning content to help you continue practising your language skills on your Coffee Break. Just search for Coffee Break Swedish on your favourite social media platform.

Vi ses!

facebook.com/coffeebreakswedish

twitter.com/cbswedish

instagram.com/coffeebreaklanguages

youtube.com/@coffeebreakswedish

tiktok.com/@coffeebreaklanguages

NOTES

NOTES

NOTES

NOTES

NOTES

ALSO BY COFFEE BREAK LANGUAGES

Do you have a friend or family member who is learning a different language? Our *50 Coffee Breaks* series also includes books in English, French, Italian, German and Spanish, available both in paperback and as ebooks.

Just visit fiftycoffeebreaks.com.

See you soon, **à bientôt, a presto, bis bald** and **¡hasta pronto!**